2008 X15 (2018)
20 (2021)

D1509525

THE LAST DAY

THE LAST DAY

WRATH, RUIN, AND REASON
IN THE GREAT LISBON EARTHQUAKE OF 1755

NICHOLAS SHRADY

VIKING

VIKING
Published by the Penguin Group
Penguin Group (USA) Inc., 375 Hudson Street, New York, New York 10014, U.S.A.
Penguin Group (Canada), 90 Eglinton Avenue East, Suite 700, Toronto, Ontario,
Canada M4P 2Y3 (a division of Pearson Penguin Canada Inc.)
Penguin Books Ltd, 80 Strand, London WC2R 0RL, England
Penguin Ireland, 25 St. Stephen's Green, Dublin 2, Ireland
(a division of Penguin Books Ltd)
Penguin Books Australia Ltd, 250 Camberwell Road, Camberwell, Victoria 3124,
Australia (a division of Pearson Australia Group Pty Ltd)
Penguin Books India Pvt Ltd, 11 Community Centre,
Panchsheel Park, New Delhi–110 017, India
Penguin Group (NZ), 67 Apollo Drive, Rosedale, North Shore 0632, New Zealand
(a division of Pearson New Zealand Ltd)
Penguin Books (South Africa) (Pty) Ltd, 24 Sturdee Avenue, Rosebank,
Johannesburg 2196, South Africa

Penguin Books Ltd, Registered Offices: 80 Strand, London WC2R 0RL, England

First published in 2008 by Viking Penguin, a member of Penguin Group (USA) Inc.

1 3 5 7 9 10 8 6 4 2

Grateful acknowledgment is made for permission to reprint an excerpt from "Het Verheerlykte en Vernederde Portugal" by F. De Haes, translated by Theo D'haen, in "On How
Not to Be Lisbon If You Want to Be Modern—Dutch reactions to the Lisbon earthquake"
by Theo D'haen, European Review 14, no. 3, July 2006. By permission of Theo D'haen.

LIBRARY OF CONGRESS CATALOGING-IN-PUBLICATION DATA
Shrady, Nicholas.
The last day : wrath, ruin, and reason in the great Lisbon earthquake of 1755 /
Nicholas Shrady.
p. cm
Includes bibliographical references and index.
ISBN 978-0-670-01851-2
1. Lisbon Earthquake, Portugal, 1755.   I. Title.
DP762.S57 2008
946.9'42033—dc22   2007042783

Printed in the United States of America
Designed by Nancy Resnick

FOR EVA

ACKNOWLEDGMENTS

My most sincere thanks to the following individuals and institutions for their generosity and thoughtfulness in helping me to write this book: Eva Ortega Adell, Christy Fletcher and Emma Parry, David Cashion, Michael and Shelley Carr, George Wright, Dexter Hodges, Gregorio Sánchez, Christopher and Lesley Cooke, José Sarmento de Matos, Anne Chaudoir, Michael Millard, Karl Fuchs, João Macarenhas Mateus, the British Library, the Biblioteca Olissiponense, the Biblioteca Gerald a Fundação Calouste Gulbenkian, the British Historical Society of Portugal, the Public Records Office (London), the Museu da Cidade, the Câmara Municipal de Lisboa, and the Arquivo Histórico Municipal de Lisboa, National Information Service for Earthquake Engineering, University of California, Berkeley.

CONTENTS

Acknowledgments vii

ONE: ALL SAINTS' DAY 3

TWO: ORDER OUT OF CHAOS 25

THREE: TAKING STOCK 49

FOUR: ALIS UBBO . . . OLISIPO . . . AL-USHBUNA . . . LISBOA 63

FIVE: A GOLDEN AGE, OF SORTS 81

SIX: THE PREACHER AND THE PHILOSOPHER 113

SEVEN: LIKE A PHOENIX FROM THE FLAMES 147

EIGHT: ENLIGHTENMENT AT ANY PRICE 169

EPILOGUE 203

Notes 211

Bibliography 215

Index 221

Earth shivered and shook, the very foundations of the hills quailed and quaked before his anger; smoke went up before his indignant presence, and a consuming fire; burning coals were kindled as he went.

—2 Kings 22:8–9

I was washing the tea things when the Dreadful affair hapned. itt began like the rattleing of Coaches, and the things befor me danst up and downe upon the table, I look about me and see the Walls a shakeing and a falling down then I up and took to my heells, with Jesus in my mouth.

—The nun Kitty Witham in a letter to her mother in England

Later, when the earth had ceased to tremble and a fine dust of ages had settled over Lisbon like a shroud, when the sea had spilled back into the placid expanse of the Tagus estuary and the last embers of an all-consuming fire had been extinguished, only then would the survivors come to dwell on the prophecies. For as long as anyone could remember, soothsayers and diviners, pamphleteers and prognosticators, clerics and ascetics had been preaching unequivocal doom for the Portuguese capital. The signs and portents, they insisted, were varied if unmistakable—a rash of stillborn infants, a comet streaking the heavens, the feverish dreams of a cloistered nun, a vision of avenging angels hovering over the city—and they all pointed to Lisbon's destruction at the hands of a wrathful God. The admonitions had Lisbon expiring variously by drought, plague, famine, invasion, earthquakes, tempests, a proliferation of vermin, and the return of the Spanish overlords, but the most common chastisement was always by flood (as for Noah) or fire (as for Sodom). From the pulpits came a torrent of sermons that took the city to task for a litany of sins. Never mind that the Portuguese were demonstrably devout, pious beyond reason, and the staunch guardians of an arch Roman Catholicism. Lisbon, railed a zealous clergy, had become steeped in iniquity and its people mired in moral turpitude through the triumph of wantonness, greed, sloth, corruption, and worst of all, the venal proximity of heretical foreign Protestants! The days of reckoning were close at hand; woe to those who failed to heed the call to repentance! And then the preachers cited liberally from the book of the Apocalypse: "Alas! Alas! Thou great city, thou mighty city, Babylon! In one hour has thy judgement come. Alas, alas, for the great city that was clothed in fine linen, in purple and scarlet, bedecked with gold, with jewels, and with pearls! In one hour all this wealth has been laid waste."

This is what people would remember, the Apocalypse, for that is what the first days of November resembled more than anything else, as earth, sea, and fire conspired to lay waste to Lisbon.

CHAPTER ONE

ALL SAINTS' DAY

They had scarcely set foot in the town [Lisbon] when they felt the earth tremble under their feet; the sea rose in foaming masses in the port and smashed the ships which rode at anchor. Whirlwinds of flame and ashes covered the streets and squares; the houses collapsed, the roofs were thrown upon the foundations, and the foundations were scattered; thirty thousand inhabitants of every age and sex were crushed under the ruins . . .

"What can be the sufficient reason for this phenomenon?" said Pangloss.

"It is the Last Day!" cried Candide.

—François-Marie Arouet, Voltaire, *Candide, or Optimism*

It was the first of November 1755. All Saints' Day dawned crisp and cloudless, and white-stone Lisbon lay mantled in a keen autumnal light that cast elongated shadows from the summits of the surrounding hills to the banks of the river Tagus. A faint northeast breeze carried ribbons of chimney smoke from the cooking fires warming the kitchens of the city, spiraling aloft into a cerulean sky, and caused the standards raised on the battlements of the tenth-century Moorish-built Castelo de São Jorge, which kept vigil over Lisbon, to scarcely waver. In the harbor formidable Portuguese men-of-war and frigates, their gun portholes latched, and a flotilla of merchant ships flying flags from England, the Netherlands, France, Spain, Denmark, Malta, Venice, and Hamburg bobbed faintly on limpid waters. To even the most jaundiced observer, Lisbon seemed like a place blessed.

It was blessed geography, in fact, that had given rise to Lisbon. Spread over seven verdant hills on the northern shore of the Tagus, close to the Atlantic but sheltered from the open sea, and backed by the jagged peaks of Sintra, the beauty of the place was already grasped by the Phoenicians, who first settled the area around 1000 B.C. Greeks and later Carthaginians established trading communities here, and later still the Romans elevated Olisipo, as they called the port, to a *municipium*. The Visigoths made it a citadel, as did the Moors. By the time Lisbon became the capital of a fledgling Portugal in 1260, the city already possessed a downright hoary past. But it was the advent of overseas conquest, exploration, and trade during the fifteenth and sixteenth centuries, the so-called Age of Discovery, that gave Lisbon the air of one of Europe's most opulent and vibrant capitals. Explorers such as Prince Henry the Navigator, Vasco da Gama, and scores of other intrepid mariners set sail from Lisbon on their imperial voyages for God, Glory, and Gold (not necessarily in that order), and it was to Lisbon's quays that they returned from Asia, Africa, and Brazil, laden with the exotic fruits of an empire, including spices, gold, rare woods, arms, sugar, tobacco, and, infamously, West African slaves. When a veritable mother lode of gold and profuse diamond deposits were discovered in Brazil at the end of the seventeenth century, a good many contemporaries believed that the Portuguese had stumbled upon the true El Dorado. Portugal, a country that was diminutive, geographically remote, and almost wholly agricultural, became justly renowned for its gilt. "Merchants who have lived in Portugal inform us," wrote John Wesley, the English divine and founder of Methodism, "that the King had a large building filled with diamonds; and more gold stored up, coined and uncoined, than all the other princes of Europe together."[1]

Despite the splendid if ill-gotten bounty of an empire, however, by the middle of the eighteenth century, most of Portugal was still wallowing in nearly medieval destitution. King João V, who fancied himself a Portuguese version of Louis XIV, *Le Roi Soleil*, was entitled to his "royal fifth" of all gold and diamonds, and he lavished the treasure on the Catholic Church and the royal family. The Portuguese nobility wielded most of the monopolies on imports; and foreign merchants, most notably the British, controlled the lion's share of the highly profitable re-export market. The goldsmiths of Italy and the diamond cutters of the Netherlands gained more from the treasures of Brazil than any Portuguese. Had Portugal fostered a true merchant class and emergent industries as did, for example, their diligent Dutch rivals, the country would have thrived, but as it was, Portugal was unable to adequately feed and clothe the populace from its own resources and was obliged to import, among other necessities, wheat, cloth, and, astonishingly, fish. It didn't seem to matter, not as long as the Brazilian bonanza continued unabated.

Portuguese colonial possessions stretched from Brazil to Macau, but Lisbon was the de facto capital and nerve center of this overextended empire. By 1750 the city's population had grown to a quarter million, and the port was one of the busiest in Europe, but Lisbon was in irreversible decline. The rapacity of the Crown, the nobility, and the foreign merchants prevented much trickling down of revenues from foreign trade and commerce. Industry was almost nonexistent, and the general level of education was so low that clerks and accountants had to be imported from abroad to work in the great trading companies. The city had its fair share of palaces and noble residences, built of a pristine white stone for which Lisbon was famous, but the majority of the people lived in rather cramped quarters in approximately twenty thousand mostly ramshackle houses of adobe, brick, and wood. Some of the streets were cobbled, others unpaved, but all were routinely sullied with the refuse that the inhabitants were accustomed to tossing from their windows. Indeed, public sanitation had been better under the Romans and the Moors. To dodge the filth, the well-to-do were borne about in sedan chairs. At nightfall the city gates were closed, and few ventured out into the unlit and unpoliced streets;

those who did were likely to tuck a pistol or a dagger beneath their knee-length capes.

Still, for all these blemishes and shortcomings, life in Lisbon was remarkably agreeable, especially by eighteenth-century standards. Although summers could be stifling, the climate was generally mild and wholesome. The city was surrounded by farms, vineyards, and orchards that provided fresh produce for the central market, which was adorned with brilliant *azulejo* tiles and reputed to be immaculately clean. Red wine was cheap, if a bit rough, and sardines, a Portuguese staple, were plentiful. There was opera for the noble and patrician classes and more bawdy theater for the commoners, but a stroll in the emblematic Rossio square was a diversion enjoyed by all. Religious feasts and festivals marked the calendar and provided a sense of cohesion and continuity to everyone save the city's beleaguered Jews and Muslims. Foreign visitors were apt to describe Lisbon as an "African city" on account of the preponderance of slaves and immigrants from Portugal's colonies in Brazil and Paraguay, Mozambique and Angola, the Azores and Goa, Macau and Malacca, but slaves notwithstanding, the racial mix gave Lisbon a patina of worldliness.

Many Portuguese may have still regarded themselves flatteringly, in the mirror of the times, as the heroic descendants of the Great Mariners, a race that God had blessed with the gifts and rewards of discovery. But in truth it had been centuries since Portugal had discovered much more than loot, and the new revelations of the Enlightenment that were captivating the rest of Europe— that is to say, empiricism, the inductive method, and a pronounced hostility toward religious superstition—and that were the true discoveries of the times had been all but stifled in Portugal by a powerful and archaic Catholic Church. In a popular travel guide from the period entitled *Description de la ville de Lisbonne,* published anonymously in Paris in 1730, the author provided a sobering portrait of the locals: "The Portuguese are large, well built and robust, but most of them are rather indolent, partly because of the climate and still more because of the intermixture with blacks, which is quite common. They are jealous to the highest degree, secretive, vengeful, sarcastic, vain and presumptuous without cause, since most of them have only a very mediocre education . . . They are also faithful friends, generous, charitable."[2]

But what most struck the author of the *Description* and nearly every other first-time traveler to Lisbon was the unparalleled piety of the inhabitants. From the pulpit, Lisbon's clergy were forever portraying the city as a sink of iniquity, but these were the splenetic words of God-fearing churchmen and hardly the true stamp of the city. If the sheer quantity of sanctified venues was the measure, Lisbon seemed the closest one could come to an earthly City of God. In addition to the twelfth-century patriarchal cathedral, Lisbon counted more than 40 parish churches, several nonparochial churches, 121 oratories, 90 convents, and close to 150 assorted religious brotherhoods and societies. In Lisbon, spires rose like copses of trees, and domes and cupolas resembled lofty hillocks; it was an ecclesiastical geography centuries in the making, a landscape of piety and devotion that marked the social and spiritual life of its inhabitants. Indeed, one could hardly take a step in the city without encountering a church, a wayside cross, a saintly shrine, or a Madonna rendered in polychrome *azulejos*.* Religious processions of penitents were commonplace;

---

*Upon arrival in the port of Lisbon, foreign ship captains were obliged to sign an oath pledging that they and their crews would doff their hats when meeting men of the cloth, kneel at every elevation of the Host, and "in no way insult the Cross, wherever set up, by making [water], but however urgent their necessities may be, will retain the same till a proper and lawful distance."

the worship of sacred relics, often of dubious provenance, was widespread; and miraculous tales of divine intervention, saintly guidance, and prayers ineffably fulfilled were part of the public record. Of a population of approximately 250,000, more than 10 percent of Lisbon's residents were members of a religious order.* And while King José I, who bore the title of *Fidelissimus*, or "Most Faithful," was considered to embody a measure of the divine and ruled over an absolute monarchy, Portugal often resembled nothing so much as a well-entrenched theocracy. The Catholic Church, the country's oldest institution and its principal land and property owner, wielded a monopoly on education, the confessional, hospitals, and the tribunals of the justly feared Holy Office of the Inquisition—that is to say, knowledge, conscience, health, and ecclesiastical law—and ostensibly ruled the life of the average Portuguese subject.

To foreign visitors and residents, especially Protestants and those of a more enlightened bent, the rites and rituals of the Portuguese smacked of popery, idol worship, and inveterate superstition, and inspired reactions ranging from mockery to general loathing. In the spring of 1753 George Whitefield, the tireless evangelist of the Great Methodist Awakening in Britain, found himself waylaid in Lisbon with twenty-two orphans in tow, while en route to a preaching stint in colonial Georgia. In letters to his Methodist brethren in London, Whitefield described with undisguised revulsion some of the religious ceremonies to which he was a witness. "One night, about ten o'clock, I saw a train of near two hundred penitents, making a halt, and kneeling in the street,

---

*In all of Portugal the clergy numbered roughly 200,000 out of a population of three million, making it "more priest ridden than any other country in the world with the possible exception of Tibet," according to the historian Charles Boxer.

whilst a friar, from a high cross, with a crucifix in his hand, was preaching to them and the populace, with great vehemence." As the procession made its way through the night-veiled streets, the penitents lashed themselves with whips and chains, beat their breasts in lament, and chanted *Penitência!* "All were bare-footed," Whitefield wrote, "and all had long heavy chains fastened to their ankles, which, when dragged along the street, made a dismal rattling." Whitefield's response to such a medieval scene of self-mortification was thoroughly apt. "O happy England!" he concluded. "O happy Methodists!"[3]

While a good deal of such public veneration was exceedingly palpable, if not inescapable, not all of it sprang from a pureness of the Christian heart. Throughout Portugal religious observance was, for all intents and purposes, mandatory, since noncompliance—a failure to attend mass or a disregard for the Sabbath and the prescribed holy days—could be denounced before the Inquisition. And lest anyone think to ignore or contradict unequivocal Catholic dogma, the Inquisition's spectacular show trials and autos-da-fé were incentive enough to maintain a conspicuous public faith.* Ecclesiastical logic was hardly lost on the multitudes that gathered in the Rossio or the Terreiro do Paço square, hard by the Royal Palace, to witness heretics, dissenters, humanists, and converted Jews suspected of practicing the old religion burn at the stake. Ever since the Holy Office of the Inquisition was established in Portugal in 1536 as a bulwark of the Counter-Reformation, the odor of sanctity had been tinged with that of

---

*The term *auto-da-fé* (also *auto-de-fé*, meaning "an act of faith") was coined by the Portuguese and refers to the ceremony in which sentences of the Holy Office of the Inquisition were read and executed. The impenitent could be condemned to prison, torture, or, in the case of the most grievous sins against the Church, the flames.

burning human flesh, and the effect made for a singularly submissive flock. The impetus to orthodoxy had less to do with freedom of conscience than with a legitimate fear of falling into the clutches of the Inquisition.

And so it was that by midmorning on November 1, 1755, with a peal of church bells beckoning the faithful, the tangled streets of Lisbon were teeming with crowds bound for their devotions. All Saints' was a solemn observance in the liturgical calendar, and the ways of Mammon were put to rest for the day. There was little activity on the habitually teeming quays; the Casa da India, seat of Portugal's international commerce and trade, was shuttered, as were the Customs Exchange and the British Factory, where members of Lisbon's thriving British merchant class gathered to press their business, sip intemperate quantities of port, complain of the ensuing bouts of gout, and calculate their windfalls. Shops and emporiums were likewise closed. In a country renowned as a bastion of Catholic orthodoxy, the central public act of the day was, predictably, holy mass. The city's elite—grandees, lesser nobles, government ministers, dignitaries of the Church, and foreign ambassadors—took to the streets in elegant horse-drawn coaches or were carried in sedan chairs borne by slaves so as to avoid the havoc of the rabble and the grime and open sewers of Lisbon's medieval lanes. Naturally, the commoners were on foot. The choice of which church to attend was customarily confined to one's parish, but on All Saints' Day many of Lisbon's citizens chose to pay homage to Vincent, the city's patron saint, and made their way to the basilica of São Vincente de Fora on the eastern edge of the capital. The original church had been built in the twelfth century to commemorate the reconquest of Lisbon from the Moors, but an entirely new edifice, begun in 1582 and designed by the architects Juan de Herrera and Filipo

Terzi, was projected in an Italianate Mannerist style. With its gleaming white marble two-story facade and imposing twin bell towers crowned by lantern turrets, the church was one of the grandest in all of Lisbon. Inside, the single nave, expansive transept, and deep main chapel were reminiscent of the Jesuits' Church of the Gesù in Rome, all architectural power employed to stir the Counter-Reformation emotions of a militant faith.

For All Saints', the pews were packed. There was standing room only in the aisles and side chapels, and the crowd spilled down the steps of the entrance and into the church square. All were turned out in their churchgoing best, each in accordance with his or her condition. The priests and their attendants at the high altar wore immaculate white vestments for the solemn feast. In the front pews, reserved for the patrician class and assorted dignitaries, there was a flourish of lace and silk, brocade and velvet finery, and noble domes crowned by powdered wigs. The legal elite and the well-to-do merchant families who followed were scarcely less adorned than their titled betters. Shopkeepers and guild men and their families wore more sensible attire and refrained from the pretensions of the wig. All the women were veiled. At the rear of the church stood the soiled and threadbare throng. The air was ripe with incense and the collective drone of prayers. Light streamed into the nave through clerestory windows, and dim votive candles and lanterns filled in the shadows.

In the choir, the priests had just begun their sonorous chant of the introit *Gaudeamus omnes in Domino, diem festum . . .* when the whole church began to pitch and sway like a ship tossed in a tempest. The great bronze bells in the twin towers rang in violent fits, their chimes muddled and flat below the deafening roar of seizing earth. Candles toppled and snuffed, stained glass shattered, saints were knocked from their pedestals, and priests and parishioners alike panicked. Dozens were crushed by falling timber and a rain of marble as columns, capitals, arches, buttresses, and massive blocks of stone crumbled. Many rushed to escape to open ground, but some refused to abandon the church and frantically prayed and begged for divine forgiveness amid the turmoil, convinced that the end, the long-heralded Apocalypse, was at hand. Those who did make it outside found the square enveloped in a cloud of dust and as dark as a moonless night. Whole blocks of houses had been reduced to rubble; chasms had swallowed lanes, and landslides had smothered alleys; carriages lay wrecked, their horses writhing in agony; and Lisboans wandered half-crazed and helpless among the dead and the dying. The cumulative cries of terror and the wailing of the injured, many caught half-buried in the debris, seemed scarcely human.

Lisbon was still reeling from the initial tremor when, several minutes after the earthquake began at approximately nine-thirty A.M., a second, far more acute shock struck. Many of the more stalwart edifices of stone and marble, such as palaces, churches, and government buildings, had survived the first shock, but their foundations had been undermined; the second shock wave brought them down like houses of cards. Surrounded by a labyrinth of ruin, no one knew where to turn. Darkness obscured the route to open ground, and mountains of rubble, some several stories tall, blocked most escapes. An account in an anonymous letter by an English witness described the fate of those caught in the calamity:

> You may guess at the prodigious havoc . . . by the single instance I am going to mention. There was a high arched passage, like one of our city gates, fronting the west door of the ancient cathedral; on the left was

the famous church of Saint Anthony and on the right some private houses, several storeys high . . . At the first shock, numbers of people, who were then passing under the arch, fled into the centre of the area; those in the two churches, as many as could possibly get out, did the same. At this instant, the arched gateway, with the fronts of the two churches and the two contiguous buildings, all inclining one towards the other with the violence of the shock, fell down and buried every soul as they were standing there crowded together.[4]

Even for many of those lucky enough to have survived the initial earthquake, the harrowing experience and trauma of the disaster were as close to a near-death experience as one could come. Thomas Chase, a twenty-six-year-old British merchant who was born in Lisbon, was in his fourth-floor bedroom when the first shock struck.

Every stone in the walls separating each from the other, and grinding, as did all the walls of the other houses, one against another, with a variety of different motions, made the most dreadful jumbling noise ears ever heard. The adjoining wall of Mr. Goddard's room fell first; then followed all the upper part of his house, and of every other, as far as I could see towards the castle; when, turning my eyes quick to the front of the room—for I thought the whole city was sinking into the earth—I saw the tops of two of the pillars meet; and I saw no more. I had resolved to throw myself upon the floor, but suppose I did not; for immediately I felt myself falling, and then, how long after I know not,

but just as if waking from a dream, with confused ideas,
I found my mouth stuffed full of something, which
with my left hand I strove to get out; and not being
able to breathe freely, struggled, till my head was quite
disencumbered from the rubbish.[5]

Chase managed to free himself from the rubble, but he was injured, in shock, and trapped in a maze of ruins.

I remained in a state of stupefaction, till the still
falling tiles and rubbish made me seek for shelter under
a small arch in the narrow wall, opposite my head. As
I lay at the bottom of this, there appeared to be a little
hole quite through it: upon my approach, and with difficulty dragging myself out of the rubbish, I found the
aperture to be much larger than I had imagined it was;
and getting in my head and arm first, by degrees pulled
my whole body after, and fell, about two feet, into a
small dark place arched over at the top, which I supposed to be only a support for the two walls; till feeling
about I found on one side a narrow passage, which led
me round a place like an oven into a little room, where
stood a Portuguese man covered with dust, who, the
moment he saw me coming that way, started back, and
crossing himself all over, cried out, as the custom is
when much surprised, "*Jesus, Mary and Joseph!* who are
you? where do you come from?" which being informed
of, he placed me in a chair; and instantly clasping his
hands together, he lifted them and his eyes toward the
ceiling, in sign of the utmost distress and concern. This
made me examine myself, which before I had not time

to do. My right arm hung down before me motionless, like a great dead weight, the shoulder being out, and the bone broken; my stockings were out to pieces, and my legs covered with wounds, the right ankle swelled to a prodigious size, with a fountain of blood spouting upwards from it: the knee also was much bruised, my left side felt as if beat in, so that I could hardly breathe: all the left side of my face was swelled, the skin beaten off, the blood streaming from it, with a great wound above, and a small one below the eye, and several bruises on my back and head.*[6]

A third and final shock struck only minutes later, but it was almost gratuitous, for Lisbon was already all but leveled. In less than a quarter of an hour Nature—or in the eyes of Lisbon's faithful, a wrathful God—had managed to largely obliterate what man had toiled for centuries to raise up. Although it was still too early to take an accounting of the calamitous loss of human life, the material devastation was all too plain to see. As survivors stood and stumbled, dazed amid the rubble, they could not find the monuments and architectural reference points of their beloved local geography.

The Paço da Ribeira, the king's palace on the waterfront, lay in ruins, as did the Casa da India, the Customs Exchange, the Opera House, and—much to the satisfaction of Protestants, Jews, and free

---

*Thomas Chase survived his injuries, but the memory of the quake stayed with him for the rest of his days. His tomb at Bromley church in Kent, England, bears the following inscription: "Sacred to the memory of THOMAS CHASE, Esq. formerly of this parish; born in the City of Lisbon, the first of November, 1729, and buried under the ruins of the same house where he first saw the light, in the ever-memorable and terrible Earthquake which befell that City, on the first of November, 1755, when, after a wonderful escape, he, by degrees, recovered from a very deplorable condition, and lived till the 20th November, 1788."

thinkers—the Palácio dos Estaus, headquarters of the Inquisition. More than twenty parish churches were utterly destroyed, as were some of the larger convents and monasteries. Scores of private palaces and townhouses, shops and warehouses, hospices and markets, were duly flattened. But the structures that suffered most were, not surprisingly, the humble dwellings, not to speak of the hovels, of Lisbon's working class and poor; these were reduced to mere heaps of dust beyond any hope of repair. The city looked, not like Lisbon, but like a twisted nightmarish version of itself. Still, as hellish as it was, the earthquake was but a prelude. As the clouds of dust and lime settled and the darkness lifted, the morning light revealed a city in flames. The candles that had illuminated Lisbon's altars and the well-stoked fires that had burned in thousands of hearths and stoves throughout the city were now blazing out of control. To make matters worse, the early morning breeze had risen to violent gusts, and the wind only fanned the flames.

What with the earth in spasms, with palaces and hovels alike collapsed all around, and with fire raging unimpeded, many of those who had gotten through the worst of the earthquake with their lives and limbs intact promptly made for the river. Terra firma being what it was, a crowd of thousands soon gathered along the waterfront hoping to find a boat or a ship to ferry them across the Tagus to more open terrain on the far shore. The scene on the quays was one of desperation as the survivors, many injured, half-clothed, and in shock, begged, bid, and fought for places on any vessel that would float. Amid the chaos, priests moved through the crowd exhorting the people to repent and offering hasty benediction; many dropped to their knees, beat their breast, and wailed or whimpered the only entreaty that the circumstances would allow: *Miserecordia, meu Deos!* Among those in the crowd was an English merchant who had dodged falling buildings, scaled and descended mountains of rubble, and fled in horror from the dead and maimed around his ruined house in the Barrio Alto to make his way to the presumed safety of the Tagus. He too was on his knees in prayer, albeit of the Protestant sort, when:

> On a sudden I heard a general outcry. The sea is coming in, we shall all be lost. Upon this, turning my eyes toward the river, which in that place is near four miles broad, I could perceive it heaving and swelling in a most unaccountable manner, as no wind was stirring. In an instant there appeared at some small distance a vast body of water, rising as it were, like a mountain, it came on foaming and roaming, and rushed toward the shore with such impetuosity that tho' we all immediately ran for our lives as fast as possible many were swept away.[7]

With the river threatening a watery grave and the city enveloped in smoke and flames, a means and route of escape proved impossible to find:

> As there now appeared at least as much danger from the sea as the land, and I scarce knew where to retire for shelter, I took a sudden resolution of returning back, with my clothes all dripping, to the area of St. Paul's. Here I stood some time, and observed the ships tumbling and tossing about, as in a violent storm. Some had broken their cables and were carried to the other side of the Tagus. Others were whirled round with incredible swiftness, several large boats were turned keel upwards and all this without any wind, which seemed very

astonishing. 'Twas at the time I am now speaking of, that the fine new quay, all built of rough marble, at an immense charge, was entirely swallowed up, with all the people on it, who had fled thither for safety, and had reason to think themselves out of danger in such a place. At the same time a great number of boats and small vessels, anchored near it, all likewise full of people who had retired thither for the same purpose, were swallowed up, as in a whirlpool, and never more appeared.[8]

Three tsunamis would slam the Lisbon waterfront on All Saints'; they rose up at approximately eleven A.M., ninety minutes after the earthquake began, and did their damage in a span of less than five minutes. The force of the waves was such that they sank all but the most formidable ships; washed away warehouses replete with stocks; collapsed quays; ravaged shipyards; and drowned an untold multitude. For days the surface of the Tagus, which soon grew placid once again, was afloat with wreckage and the pale, bloated corpses of those who had sought refuge at the riverside.

The king had risen at dawn on All Saints'. José I, Queen Maria Ana Victória, and their four daughters heard mass early in the royal chapel at the Paço da Ribeira and duly prayed for all the saints, with special invocations to São Jorge, or Saint George, patron of Portugal. Following the service, the royal family climbed into gilded carriages and drove west along the road that skirted the river, bound for the royal retreat at Belém. In their wake followed a courtly and chaotic entourage of clergy, confessors, stewards, chamberlains, privies, ladies-in-waiting, and lesser attendants. The princesses had implored their father to spend the feast day in the countryside, and the king, a monarch fond of bucolic pursuits, especially the hunt, gladly obliged. The day looked to be magnificent. The carriages rattled over cobblestones toward Belém, four miles from the city center. Church bells sounded from every quarter; the crowds in the street cheered, doffed their hats, and bowed low to the fleeting royal procession. The king, surrounded by his beloved if heirless family, was in exceedingly good cheer. Moored in the harbor were the Portuguese fleets from India and Brazil, recently arrived laden with pepper and tobacco, gold and precious stones, sugar and human cargo, one-fifth of the revenues from which was destined for the royal coffers. There seemed every reason to be cheerful.

The royal entourage had scarcely settled in at the king's compound in Belém when the first shock of the earthquake caught the monarchs in their respective chambers: the princesses in the oratory, and assorted courtiers, retainers, priests, and servants in various corners of the palace. Royals, nobles, men of the cloth, and plebeians all scrambled as best they could—and, one presumes, with little deference to social hierarchy—to open ground in the garden. There was panic and hysteria, shock and confusion, but astonishingly, the entire lot emerged not only with their lives, but without so much as a scratch. In a letter to her mother in Madrid, dated the fourth of November, Queen Maria Ana Victória described the royal family's brush with disaster:

> My very dear Mother,
>   This letter has been dispatched by a special courier of the King, who recommended that it be sent immediately, before you should receive any false news that might cause you suffering.
>   We are all alive and in good health, may God be a thousand times praised . . .

At 9:45 on Saturday morning, we felt a most terrible tremor of the earth; we fled outside with immense difficulty since we could barely remain standing. I ran for the Arabic staircase, where, without the help of God, I would certainly have broken my head or legs for I could hardly proceed and was consumed by fear, as you can imagine, convinced as I was that my final hour had arrived. The King joined me soon after, for he had fled from the other side of the house. My daughters had been in the oratory and were able to join us later. Apart from their [the princesses'] quarters, which were slightly ruined, they suffered nothing, thank God, but since then we are all residing in the large garden . . .

Lisbon has been almost completely destroyed and many people have been crushed to death, among them, poor Perelada [Spanish ambassador to Lisbon], and to make matters worse, a fire erupted and consumed a large part of the city, there being no one willing to return to extinguish it. Our palace was half destroyed, but what remained went up in flames along with everything inside; nevertheless, the women were saved.

Forgive me, my dear Mother, for not relating more details, but our state and the confusion does not allow me time to do so. May God have mercy on us, we have been spared. May God be praised thousands of times. There exist cases of enormous tragedy and universal desolation.

I beg of you, with the utmost humility, to pray to God that He continue to have mercy on us . . .

We bow humbly at your feet, my dear Mother, and ask God to keep and protect you from misfortune.[9]

Although the effects of the quake were far less destructive in Belém, the king nonetheless refused to enter the country palace and ordered tents to be pitched among the immaculate parterres in the garden. Soon a bewildered José I was ensconced in a make-shift tented court, accompanied by his family, a clutch of confessors, and a swelling rank of dazed and largely ineffectual courtiers. Priests exhorted the royal family to pray for the intercession of the saints and beseech the Almighty for the forgiveness of their sins, but the king was disconsolate and paralyzed with fear. If God had delivered such pernicious divine justice while the faithful were in the midst of their devotions on All Saints' Day, had the Almighty not forsaken them? "Wherefore hath the Lord done thus unto this great city?" True, the king and his family had so far survived the cataclysm, a fact that might well be interpreted as an act of divine providence, a sign that José I was destined to perse-vere and rule.

Faced with the monumental scope of the destruction, how-ever, the king, aged forty and inclined more to the high-flown registers of the opera and the exhilaration of the hunt than to the gritty business of ruling his kingdom, was at a conspicuous loss. Messengers arrived throughout the morning bearing ever more explicit accounts of the infernal scenes of terror and ruin, the in-calculable death toll, and the coming of the Apocalypse. At eleven A.M. the king and his court watched in horror as the tsuna-mis battered the shore at Belém. Some talked of fleeing the stricken city for the supposed safety of the interior or, more auda-cious still, of moving the capital north to Coimbra or perhaps to Rio de Janeiro. Lisbon, after all, was no more. All the while the priests persisted in their prayers; the princesses wept unabated; and the king, sullen and impotent, did precisely what no monarch should ever do: he cowered.

In the midst of this less-than-regal display of inertia and despair that threatened to abandon Lisbon to providence and the elements, one of the king's secretaries of state, Sebastião José de Carvalho e Melo, better known to history by his later title of the Marquês de Pombal, arrived. Ushered before the king, Carvalho was shocked by the scene of confusion and pious invocations and by the sight of his monarch manifestly lost in anguish. The exchange that ensued was momentous, if perhaps apocryphal, but it defined the response to the crisis with the precision of an aphorism.

"What is to be done to meet this infliction of divine justice?" cried the king.

"Bury the dead and feed the living," Carvalho replied.

The utterance, both commanding and glaringly sensible, was just what the foundering king wished to hear. Mired as he was in the religious literalism fostered by his confessors, José I suddenly regarded Carvalho as heaven-sent, an agent of providence who had arrived at the kingdom's darkest hour. After all, Carvalho too had survived the quake; indeed, his house on the Rua do Século in the Barrio Alto, where he was residing when the disaster struck, was scarcely affected (although skeptics pointed out that neither were the brothels on the Rua Suja). If, according to the king's logic, Carvalho had been spared, it was because God saw fit to make him His instrument and deliver Lisbon from the inferno. In one of the only coherent decisions he made during the crisis, José I promptly vested his minister with the authority to confront the catastrophe by whatever means he saw fit. Carvalho took leave of the king and court, climbed into his carriage, and hastened back to the place that was once Lisbon.

CHAPTER TWO

ORDER OUT OF CHAOS

His Majesty, assisted by the Secretary of State, Sebastião José Carvalho e Melo, a wise, zealous and active minister, took the necessary measures to help, relieve and safeguard the people, and for the advantageous re-establishment of Lisbon.

Everything was wise solutions, correct actions and blessed laws.

—Joaquim José Moreira de Mendonça, História universal
dos terramotos . . . com uma narraçam individual
do terramoto do primeiro de Novembro de 1755

In truth, Sebastião José de Carvalho e Melo was an improbable deliverer. His family belonged not to the aristocracy, from whose ranks the king's ministers and confidants were habitually drawn, but rather to the country gentry, or *fidalgos*, a class wedged uneasily between the upper bourgeoisie and the lesser nobility. Given the rigidity of Portugal's consummately stratified society, in which nobility of blood was much prized and the fate of commoners was nearly feudal, Carvalho's rise to the post of secretary of state was nothing short of astonishing; he achieved it by a combination of unbridled ambition, an uncanny political instinct, and two exceedingly advantageous marriages.

Sebastião José's father, Manuel de Carvalho e Ataide, held a commission in a royal cavalry regiment and moved to Lisbon with his wife just prior to his son's birth in 1699. The future minister's upbringing, like that of his five younger siblings, was neither deprived nor privileged, but he did benefit from one influence that was altogether extraordinary for the times. Between 1717 and 1720, at an age when Sebastião José was perhaps most impressionable and, no doubt, contemplating his future in the world, the family's house on the Rua do Século served as a meeting place for the Academia dos Ilustrados, an informal group of enlightened intellectuals and progressive, civic-minded men that was sponsored by Carvalho's uncle. At a time when new ideas rarely reached Portugal without first undergoing the scrutiny of the Inquisition and its censors, the activities of the Academia dos Ilustrados were not only exceptional but positively dangerous. The group, which included the Conde de Ericeira, future director of the Academia Real da História Portuguesa, provided a forum for discussion of many of the philosophical, political, and scientific revelations that were gaining ground in northern Europe—the Cartesian method, enlightened absolutism, Newtonian physics. These ideas were otherwise thoroughly absent from Portugal on account of ecclesiastical censure and an inveterate mentality among the general populace that remained forbiddingly medieval. Sebastião José was a silent observer at these gatherings, but they instilled in him a taste for public discourse, a penchant for novel ideas, and a sense of civic duty.

Carvalho entered the venerable University of Coimbra to study law and so to accede through the legal profession to the vaunted status of *noblesse de robe*. The university, however, was a fortress of conservatism, where humanism, the Reformation, and the revolutionary discoveries in the natural sciences had long been categorically banned. Having experienced the relatively informal and spirited forums of the Academia dos Ilustrados, Carvalho found the hierarchy and discipline of academic life, and Coimbra's obsolete syllabus with its emphasis on canon law, to be stultifying. His professors, in turn, found their charge impetuous, outspoken, and devoid of the proper decorum that the law required. Carvalho left Coimbra without completing his studies and enlisted in the army. Military life, however, especially for those of the rank and file, was no match for Carvalho's ambition; after a brief stint he left the service with the lowly rank of private. Returning to his native Lisbon, Carvalho lived as a young man about town and became a

member of one of the rowdy but innocuous youth gangs, or "Mohocks," that roamed the streets. He went by the moniker "the Oak,"
a literal translation of his surname, on account of his towering physical stature. Sebastião José may have been something of a ruffian, but
he seems to have aroused the fancy of the ladies of Lisbon and of
those decidedly not the common sort. In 1723, at the age of twenty-
four, he eloped with and married Teresa de Noronha e Bourbon, a
widow ten years his senior who belonged to one of the most distinguished families in Portugal. For the bride's family, the union was a
scandal, but for Carvalho, Teresa was, so to speak, a singular catch.

The couple set up house on an estate in Soure, south of Coimbra, and Carvalho, now cushioned by a handsome dowry, took up
the gentlemanly study of history and politics. Through a well-
placed uncle, who was archpriest at the patriarchal cathedral in
Lisbon, Carvalho gained an audience with Cardinal Mota, a minister to King João V. It was Carvalho's first introduction to the
powerful corridors of the court, and by all accounts, he made a favorable impression. Shortly thereafter he was made a member of
the Academia Real de História Portuguesa (the Conde de Ericeira
undoubtedly played a part), and the king commissioned him to
write a history of the Portuguese monarchs. Nothing ever came of
the history, but Carvalho became a conspicuous fixture at court,
taking an active part in debates regarding issues of national legis-
lation and international trade. He proved at once persuasive and
informed and seems to have shed, at least in the aura of the court,
the more volatile instincts of his youth.

In 1739 he was sent to London as minister plenipotentiary with
the express mission of redressing the historic trade imbalance that
plagued Portugal's commercial relations with Britain, for centuries
the country's staunchest military and mercantile ally. Less than
three months after the couple's arrival in London, however, Teresa

became ill and died suddenly and inexplicably, leaving Carvalho devastated but also the sole beneficiary of a vast estate. He tempered the personal loss by immersing himself obsessively in his professional duties, achieving, among other things, more favorable conditions for Portuguese merchants in London, and an end to the impunity with which the British merchant fleet operated in Portugal and her colonies. Carvalho's years in London gave him a certain urbanity and polish that he would never have acquired in Lisbon. He negotiated directly with the Duke of Newcastle, the great Whig statesman who was then secretary of state; and although he moved in rarefied diplomatic circles, he also sought out and conferred with the large Portuguese Jewish exile community in London.

Above all, he read the writings of Jean-Baptiste Colbert on mercantilism, Thomas Hobbes on absolutism, John Locke on constitutional monarchy, and Isaac Newton on natural philosophy. King João V personally gave him the task of acquiring a collection of Hebrew bibles, religious tracts, histories of the Jews, and books of Jewish customs and rituals for the royal library in Lisbon. This was a macabre request from a monarch who witnessed and condoned Jews being burned at the stake before the royal palace, but João V was both a bigot and a bibliophile. The minister dutifully did the king's bidding.

In 1745 he was appointed the Portuguese ambassador to Vienna. In the Austrian capital Carvalho met his second wife, Leonara Ernestine Daun, daughter of Count Leopold Joseph von Daun, and in wealth, influence, and beauty, she was an even better catch than Teresa. Carvalho's new bride was a personal friend of the Austrian princess who had become Queen Maria Ana of Portugal, and when King João V became incapacitated by senility, the queen assumed the regency. Not surprisingly, a place was soon found for Carvalho in Lisbon; in 1749 he was recalled to Portugal to assume the post of secretary of state for foreign affairs. Carvalho's appointment was the result not of his wife's influence on the queen, although it surely helped his cause, but of an explicit recommendation by Luís da Cunha, an eminent diplomat, adviser to King José I, and mentor to Carvalho. Da Cunha too had served as a minister in London, and both men shared a vision of the profound need for social, economic, and political reform in Portugal. In his *Testamento político*, a lengthy letter to the king on political exigencies and the art of statecraft, the diplomat proposed Carvalho for secretary of state on the basis of "a patient, speculative and diffuse nature that is in agreement with the nation."[1] From impoverished gentry to one of the most powerful appointments in the realm: by any measure Carvalho's rise had been meteoric.

One may be tempted to say that all of Carvalho's life had been preparation for handling the 1755 quake and its aftermath, but no manner of life experience could have adequately prepared anyone for such a catastrophe. Still, Carvalho seems to have leaped at the opportunity to confront the chaos of the quake. Nothing in his official capacity as secretary of state for foreign affairs obliged him to assume a conspicuous role. In the most profound sense Carvalho rose to an occasion that was nothing if not insurmountable, displaying the qualities of selflessness and audacity that are the indispensable conditions of a hero. Indeed, who but a hero would descend knowingly and unswervingly into the inferno?

As Carvalho approached Lisbon from Belém at midafternoon, he looked out the window of his carriage to see great plumes of smoke rising from every corner of the capital. Hundreds of separate fires, fanned by the continuing winds from the northeast, had grown into a conflagration. And the exodus had begun. The streets, or what remained of them, were swarming with survivors, some half-naked, caked in blood and dust, crazed and raving, all

frantically trying to flee the city for the open countryside. Many
were clutching crucifixes and saintly icons and whatever meager
possessions they had managed to drag from the rubble. The crowd,
as is so often the case in general calamities, was forcibly heteroge-
neous, comprising patricians and the destitute, children and the
elderly, cloistered nuns and mothers bearing infants, savvy merchants and foreign dignitaries, servants and their masters. Titles,
pedigrees, wealth, and social standing were suddenly hopelessly
irrelevant. The natural disaster had cast them all together as no
human endeavor could in a common rush for survival. The earthquake had become the great indisputable leveler. The flight was
at once natural—deriving from an all-too-human instinct for
self-preservation—and in some instances downright disgraceful.
Among the crush were soldiers and officers who had abandoned
their posts, clergy who had turned away from their flocks, and un-
injured men strong enough but little disposed to wage a rescue effort, fight the fires, or even provide succor to the injured and dying.
Some of those who were too maimed to move or were buried in the
debris were left to their fate and the encroaching flames. The exodus was made worse by a rumor, not unfounded, that the fire would
soon envelop the Castelo de São Jorge, ignite the gunpowder magazine, and cause an explosion that would deal Lisbon her final
death blow. Nor did the persistent tremors that continued to rattle
the city throughout the day do much to ease the pandemonium.
For many, flight seemed the only sensible course.

Not everyone, however, was giving up the city, not just yet.
Hundreds of common criminals, army deserters,* and slaves had

---

*Seven years after the end of the War of the Austrian Succession (1740–48)
army deserters, principally French and Spanish, were still languishing in Portuguese prisons.

escaped through breaches that the earthquake had opened at the Cadeia do Limoeiro and Cadeia da Galé prisons, and many readily took to pillage, arson, and murder. The churches, private houses, and shops that remained standing were set upon by marauding gangs in search of coin and treasure. Eyewitness accounts describe scenes of primitive criminality but also of valor. The experience of one Lisbon merchant was telling:

> Scarce had the Shaking ceased, when a Gang of remorseless Villains began to plunder the Houses that were deserted, for the Inhabitants fled they knew not whither, lest the Buildings should fall on their Heads; as soon as possible, proper Officers were ordered to seize on the Plunderers, and to fire on them in case of Resistance. I happened to be passing by at a Time when the Officers were entering a House in order to seize a Gang, who were stripping it of all they could lay their Hands on; the robbers were alarmed at the Officers approach, and one of them, coming to a Chamber Window, presented a kind of Blunderbuss, swore vehemently, that the first Person who presumed to enter was a dead Man on the Instant: There are, says he, Ten of us, all brave Fellows like myself, therefore, Gentlemen, I advise you to walk off for your own Sakes. This indeed, appeared to be only an Artifice, for the Officers, not in the least intimidated by his Threats, rushed into the House, and attempted to seize him, but he made a stout Resistance, placing himself in a Corner, where it was impossible for more than one to attack him at a Time, he killed one of the Officers, and wounded another in the Breast in a very dangerous Manner, The Third, however, disarmed

him, and he was immediately seized, conveyed to Prison, and executed the next Day.[2]

It was soon tragically clear to Carvalho that he had far more to do than simply "bury the dead and feed the living." The destruction of Lisbon was biblical in proportion, and the human losses and suffering were beyond any reckoning. Fire raged unimpeded, and there was little hope of any effective countermeasures since the city lacked a proper fire brigade and the private citizens who were customarily marshaled to fight the flames were in flight. All but the widest streets were clogged with debris, and enough rubble filled the labyrinthine alleys, passageways, and stairways that traced many of the city's oldest quarters to form an impenetrable barrier. Those who chose to remain in the less devastated areas of the city in order to protect their houses and businesses were at the mercy of the mob.

Before he could do anything to organize food supplies for the survivors or to arrange for the burial of the untold thousands of victims, Carvalho had to establish order. He sent word to the Marquês de Abrantes, commander in chief of the royal garrison, to mobilize his troops as best he could. Soldiers were dispatched to fight the fire, to attempt to rescue those buried in the rubble, and to mount guard over royal possessions,* private palaces, the Sé Cathedral, the more lavish churches and convents, the Mint (where the bullion from Brazil was stored), the Customs Exchange, and the principal trading houses; in short, anywhere that money or loot was known to exist. The troops, however, were

---

*In addition to the Paço da Ribeira palace on the waterfront and the Quinta Real de Belém, the royal family also possessed the Palácio Corte-Real, the Quinta de Alcântara, the Paço da Bemposta, the Paço de Alcáçova, and the Palácio das Necessidades.

stretched thin, and the pillaging continued for days. Reinforcements were called for, and infantry regiments from Peniche, Elvas, and Olivença and dragoons from Évora converged on Lisbon to enforce a brutal if necessary justice. By royal decree Carvalho established a cursory verbal trial and summary execution for anyone caught looting. Six new gallows were erected (especially high, it was specified) in the most conspicuous squares, and the condemned were left to hang for days as an unambiguous example of a thief's fate. Naturally there were abuses, and foreigners in particular proved easy scapegoats. Most of those executed by decree were French and Spanish deserters, but five Irishmen were also hung, as were a group of English sailors who had plundered the royal palace and chapel, and a Moorish slave who confessed to torching the city in seven places. A handful of Portuguese common criminals met the same end (including the blunderbuss-bearing murderer whom the merchant described). The effect of gallows justice was immediate: "the scandal of so many robberies soon stopped," wrote Joaquim José Moreira de Mendonça, a Portuguese chronicler and staff member of the national archives who lived through the earthquake.[3]

When the Portuguese regiments converged on Lisbon, Carvalho ordered them to round up any able men from the fleeing multitudes and march them back to the capital to work on rescue and reconstruction. The city needed every available man to retrieve the dead from the ruins, clear the streets of debris, and build temporary shelters for the thousands of homeless who were living in makeshift tents, ruined wagons, and the open air. Convincing the terror-stricken to return to a city, devastated and in flames, from which they had only narrowly escaped was no easy task; had it not been for the imperative of the sword and the bayonet, few would have willingly risked their lives for Lisbon. Perhaps in time the city would have been abandoned altogether and the capital moved to Coimbra, Évora, Oporto, or even balmy Rio de Janeiro.*

As Carvalho penetrated ruined Lisbon (in his carriage where the lanes allowed, on foot when necessary), he discovered, much to his relief, that he was not alone in the battle to save the city. Although the flight of panicked citizens was widespread, a determined few remained behind to confront the chaos. There were parish priests who stuck steadfastly with their fold to provide relief, absolution, last rites, and, when possible, the dignity of a proper Christian burial in the churchyard. Monsignor Sampaio of the Sé Cathedral, which suffered heavy damages, rescued scores from the rubble and personally buried dozens of victims. Many of those whose houses and palaces remained habitable opened their doors to the injured and the homeless. In a much-needed show of royal resolve, the illegitimate sons of João V, the princes José and Gaspar, set up a provisional shelter in the splendid halls of the Palácio Palhavã. Foreigners too, especially the British, ever unflappable in a crisis, rallied to the aid of fellow countrymen and locals alike. Abraham Castres, the British envoy extraordinary to the king of Portugal, found himself presiding over a full-blown camp in his house and garden on the Rua de Santa Marta, on the verdant northern fringe of town. In a letter to Sir Thomas Robinson, the British secretary of state and leader of the House of Commons, Castres described his domestic scene thus:

> God be praised, my house stood out the shocks, tho'
> greatly damaged; and that happening to be out of reach
> of the flames, several of my friends, burnt out of their

---

*When Napoleon's armies invaded Portugal in 1807, the royal family and court did indeed move to Rio de Janeiro.

houses, had taken refuge with me, where I have accommodated them, as well as I could, under tents in my large garden; . . . those with me at present, are the Dutch minister, his lady and their three children, with seven or eight of their servants. The rest of my company, of the better sort, consists of several merchants of this factory, who, for the most part, have lost all they had; . . . the number of dead and wounded I can give no certain account as yet; in that respect our poor factory has escaped pretty well, considering the number of houses we have here.

I have lost my good and worthy friend the Spanish Ambassador, who was crushed under his door, as he attempted to make his escape into the street. This, with the anguish I have been in . . . occasioned by the dismal accounts brought to us every instant of the accidents befalling one or other of our acquaintances among the nobility, who, for the most part, are quite underdone, has greatly affected me; but in particular the miserable objects among the lower sort of his majesty's subjects, who all fly to me for bread, and lie scattered up and down in my garden, with their wives and children. I have helped them hitherto, and shall continue to do so as long as provisions do not fail us, which I hope will not be the case, by the good orders M. de Carvalho has issued in that respect.[4]

The "good orders" to which Castres referred were crucial in avoiding the specter of starvation or, only slightly less dire, savage food riots among the survivors. In collaboration with the Marquês de Alegrete, president of the Senado da Câmara, or City Senate (another of the valiant few who refused to abandon the capital), Carvalho ordered that food-distribution points be set up in the Terreiro do Paço and Ribeira squares, where provisions that had escaped the flames, fish from the Tagus, and foodstuffs from the outlying villages were gathered under armed guard and distributed equitably. Field kitchens and open-air bread ovens were hastily set up throughout the city. Ship captains received orders to relinquish any food deemed in excess of their crews' immediate needs, and arriving ships with cargoes of grain, fish, and meat were compelled to dispose of their merchandise duty free. And in an attempt to stem profiteering, shopkeepers were obliged to respect the prices that had been in effect before the disaster; those who did not found themselves in chain gangs clearing the rubble. "With these wise decisions," wrote Moreira de Mendonça, "there was no hunger anywhere, as was feared in the first days."[5]

The fear that consumed all of Lisbon in the first days was that of an outbreak of the plague. Thousands of corpses were piled high in the streets, and more were being recovered from the ruins by the hour. The stench was appalling. But the fire, which continued to rage for the better part of a week, provided a gruesome paradox; as the flames consumed everything in their wide path, they incinerated countless decomposing corpses and thus helped to avert an epidemic. For the poor souls who were buried alive beneath the ruins, the fire spelled a particularly grisly end. Still, disposing of the remaining dead raised a delicate issue of religious custom. The Christian rite of burial in consecrated ground proved virtually impossible to fulfill, for the sheer quantity of accumulated corpses. Furthermore, the process was painstakingly slow. Carvalho petitioned the patriarch, José Cardinal Manuel da Câmara d'Atalaia, for permission to set aside the traditional practice and to bury the dead at sea without delay. The patriarch wisely offered his dispensation, and starting on November 3 barges weighed to the gunwales with the dead plied their way down the Tagus bound for the open sea, where they sank their cargo in a watery grave.

The fate of the dead was not the only issue that the minister took up with the patriarch. Of equal concern and increasingly irksome to Carvalho was the incessant preaching of apocalyptic doom that issued forth from the most fanatical among the clergy. From the first moments after the earthquake, many priests had exhorted the survivors to repent the sins that had purportedly brought on the cataclysm and to abandon damned Lisbon before God unleashed His wrath once more, as surely He would. The feverish sermons contributed significantly to the flight of the multitudes and prevented the return of inhabitants who were essential to the recovery. Carvalho wanted these zealots silenced, but he was firmly if politely rebuffed. The Church's power in Portugal was such that in a clash between royal and ecclesiastical authority, the patriarch felt no obligation to accede to the king's minister. He would issue no reprimand to the priests. It was a lesson in misplaced priorities that Carvalho would not soon forget.

Carvalho's frustration with the religious fanaticism that kept survivors focused on prayers of repentance and spiritual meditations, rather than rescue and renewal, was wholly understandable, but the refugees' reluctance to venture back to the city was hardly puzzling; the vast majority of them had no place to venture back to. On the outskirts of Lisbon tented camps had sprung up in orchards and vineyards, on monastery lands and private estates, and on the periphery of the surrounding villages. A sea of refugees was adrift, dispossessed, and utterly unsure of what the future had in store. Not even the royal family had budged from their tents in

Belém. On November 5 Abraham Castres had a royal audience in the king's makeshift dwelling:

> The roads for the first days having been impractica-
> ble, it was but yesterday I had the honour, in company
> of M. de la Calmette, of waiting upon the king of Por-
> tugal, and all the royal family, at Bellem [sic], whom we
> found encamped, none of the royal palaces being fit to
> harbour them. Tho' the loss his most faithful majesty
> has sustained on this occasion is immense, and his
> capital city is utterly destroyed, yet he received us with
> more serenity than we expected; and, among other
> things, told us, that he owed great thanks to provi-
> dence for saving his and his family's lives; and that he
> was extremely glad to see us both safe. The queen in
> her own name and all the young princesses, sent us
> word, that they were obliged to us for our attention,
> but that being under their tents, and in a dress not fit
> to appear in, they desired that for the present we would
> excuse their admitting our complements in person.[6]

The king was inclined to abandon Lisbon and move the court and capital to Coimbra. The tented life, after all, was growing tiresome; the queen and princesses were sequestered and disheart-ened; and the royal confessors seemed to concur that Lisbon's de-struction was entirely providential, like that of Nineveh or Jericho, and equally hopeless. For the king to abandon his capital and his desperate subjects in the hour of need, however, would have been rightly construed as cowardly, if not treasonous, and Carvalho tactfully told him as much. A hasty royal leave-taking, the minister also pointed out, would expose the realm to foreign powers with designs on Portugal, namely Spain, and to the merciless pirates who would gladly sack the city. In addition, the country would lose its principal port, the confidence of foreign allies and merchants, and quite possibly its far-flung and bountiful colonial empire as well. José I, not surprisingly, agreed to stay put. Had the king departed, needless to say, Carvalho's power would have been vastly diminished, for it was in José's name that his minister was able to promulgate the decrees and exert the authority to cope with the crisis. Lisbon needed Carvalho, and Carvalho needed the king in Lisbon.

On November 6 the *Gazeta de Lisboa* published a purposefully clipped report, approved by Carvalho, that summed up what was arguably the greatest natural disaster ever to have visited Europe as follows: "The first day of this month will be remembered for centuries for the earthquakes and fires which ruined a large part of the city, but we have had the good fortune to recover from the ruins the royal coffers and the majority of those belonging to private citizens." It said nothing more; not a word described the alarmingly high, if as yet uncalculated, death toll, the suffering of the injured, the plight of the survivors, or the extent of the material loss. It was a piece of understated propaganda designed to soothe the fragile nerves of the inhabitants and instill a measure of confidence.

As Carvalho's efforts put an end to lawlessness (the gallows would remain standing for months after the disaster), disposed of the dead, made food available, and kept the plague at bay, Lisbon's residents, shattered but resigned, slowly picked up the pieces of their lives that the earthquake had so suddenly and brutally crushed. Religious services were resumed amid the ruins of churches, convents, and monasteries. Merchants, priests, and families raked through the rubble and ashes to salvage what they could of their stocks, relics, personal belongings, and coin.* In time the canvas sails that had been widely used to pitch tents for the refugees were replaced by timber, procured largely from the Ribeira das Naus shipyard, to construct shelters and huts, some of them positively grand. Although Carvalho's house on the Rua do Século was perfectly habitable, for the sake of royal proximity the minister had a wooden hut built for himself hard by the king's compound at Belém. "The [hut] of the Secretary of State Sebastião José Carvalho e Melo could serve as a palace, like those of many other lords, which simultaneously shòws that the destruction was great, while the magnificence indicates the greatness of the people who live in them," observed Father Manuel Portal of the Congregation of the Oratory.[7] Naturally, the new lodgings for commoners were rather less magnificent—in fact, they were nothing more than shanties with no conveniences, modern or otherwise. Nor did the majority of refugees have an alternative. Carvalho had imposed a strict moratorium on any new building in stone until all the debris was cleared away and a new construction code and urban plan could be drawn up. The monumental process of renewal would be painfully slow and not without administrative, economic, and Church-inspired obstacles, but most survivors knew that they had been fortunate to escape the tragedy with their lives. Few families had not suffered the death of one or another loved one; some families were lost altogether. To be a Lisbon survivor was to be blessed, like the king, by providence. But survivors experienced little peace; continual tremors kept the populace in a state of perpetual anxiety. In the weeks following

---

*For years following the disaster, the silver and gold pieces used in business transactions were specified as either clean or blackened, the latter on account of the charring effects of the fire.

the quake dozens of aftershocks of various degrees of violence rocked the city, and hundreds more were reported in the first half of 1756. "Will your Earth never be quiet?" asked Sir Benjamin Keene, the British ambassador to Madrid, in a letter to Abraham Castres, dated July 31, 1756.[8] No one could possibly know.

As the days and weeks passed, coaches and ships brought news of the effects of the earthquake elsewhere, and the city learned that it was far from alone in its suffering. God had not singled out Lisbon as the exclusive source and sole recipient of his ire after all. The destruction had been far-reaching, international, even intercontinental. Setúbal, located due south of Lisbon, and Cascais to the west were both laid waste by the quake and hard hit by the tsunamis. On the western side of the Algarve coast, the destruction was nearly total. "The city of Faro has been completely destroyed," wrote the bishop of the Algarve, "as has Lagos, Silves, Vila de Loulé, Albufeira, Vila do Bisbo, Vila Nova de Portimão, Boliqueime; but above all Lagos and Albufeira, as the sea came up with such infernal fury it swept away everything that remained of the ruins of the earthquake."[9] A single edifice remained standing in Lagos, and Boliqueime was so leveled that the survivors picked up and built a new town on a nearby site. In the Spanish city of Cádiz and in coastal towns like Sanlúcar, the effects of the earthquake were minor, but those of the tsunamis were devastating and hundreds drowned.

Across the Strait of Gibraltar the waves battered the Moroccan coast from Tangiers to Agadir, and in the interior the quake did severe damage to Meknes and Fez, toppling minarets and citadels, city walls and aqueducts, and a majority of the mud-brick homes. The death toll reached well into the thousands. Not far from Meknes "the earth swallowed up a village with all its hovels, people, horses, camels, mules, cows, and other animals . . . five thousand people . . . and six thousand cavalry soldiers that were

billeted there disappeared without a trace," wrote the father cus-
todian of the Royal Monastery of Meknes.*[10] Tremors from the
earthquake were felt over an astonishingly wide stretch of Europe,
from Madrid to Lyon and Strasbourg, to Normandy and Brittany,
to Switzerland and northern Italy. The south of England noted
the shocks and reported that exceedingly high sea waves reached
London harbor. Inland waterways as far off as Scotland and Scandinavia were observed to abruptly rise and fall. At the thermal
springs in Teplitz, Bohemia, the salubrious waters grew suddenly
turbid with mud. As for the tsunamis, they rolled across the
Atlantic and hit the West Indies in the early evening, causing
heavy damage and numerous victims, especially in Barbados and
Martinique.

Despite the geographical extent of the earthquake, it was for
Lisbon that the "civilized" world would mourn. There had been a
devastating earthquake in Catania, Sicily, in 1693, in which eighteen thousand died; another in Lima, Peru, in 1746; and yet another
in Port au Prince, Haiti, in 1751, but those places were remote and,
to the collective conscience of eighteenth-century Europe at least,
largely inconsequential. Lisbon, by contrast, was a thriving capital,
the third busiest port in Europe after Amsterdam and London, and
the ideological and administrative center of power of an empire
whose vast if scattered territories extended from Brazil to the Far
East. The Portuguese monarchy had diffuse dynastic ties to Spain,
Austria, France, and England. And, of course, there were ever-vital
commercial interests to consider. Merchants and traders from Britain, the Netherlands, Hamburg, Spain, France, the Italian states,

---

*There is some question as to whether the damage in Meknes and Fez was pro-
duced by the November 1 earthquake or by subsequent quakes that were reported on November 18 and 27.

the Baltic, and Scandinavia, among others, all had money, wares, and property in the city. Turning a blind eye or a deaf ear to the plight of Lisbon was out of the question.

King George II of Britain first learned of the disaster through his ambassador in Madrid, Sir Benjamin Keene, but it was during a private audience with Portuguese envoys in London in late November that the king learned in graphic if diplomatic detail of the harrowing extent of the destruction. George II, for all his reputation as a fiscal skinflint (he took the greatest pleasure, it was said, in counting his money piece by piece, and he economized his income with the fastidiousness of a clerk), was uncharacteristically moved to munificence and immediately sent a petition to the House of Commons. "Being moved with the greatest concern for so good and faithful an ally as the King of Portugal," wrote George II, "and with the utmost compassion for the distresses to which that city and kingdom must be reduced, he desires to be enabled by the House of Commons to send such speedy and effectual relief, as may be suitable to so affecting and pressing an exigency."[11] The members of the Commons, much to their honor, voted unanimously in favor of the relief, and on November 29 the treasury allocated the then-staggering sum of 100,000 pounds, half in gold and silver, half in food and material. Much of the gold, ironically, was Portuguese, the same coin that the country used to pay its habitual trade deficit with Britain.* The remainder of the relief, ferried in six ships, consisted of 6,000 barrels of beef, 4,000 firkins of butter, 10,000 quarters each of flour and wheat, 1,000 sacks of biscuits, 1,200 sacks of rice, and shoes, pickaxes, shovels, spades, and crowbars to the value of 16,000 pounds sterling.

---

*Portuguese gold coins, bearing the effigy of King João V, were common and highly prized tender throughout Britain.

While Britain was undoubtedly the most generous and forth-coming in providing aid, it was not alone in its benevolence. Despite the long-standing enmity between Portugal and her larger, more populous, and more powerful Iberian neighbor, Spain rose above the historic differences and sent relief in the regal form of four wagonloads of gold. (Familial motives, it should be noted, were also involved, as King Fernando VI of Spain was married to King José's sister, Princess Maria Barbara.) The city of Hamburg was rather more practical and sent four shiploads of timber and clothing.

There were, however, noteworthy exceptions as well. At Versailles, the court seems to have regarded the disaster as a source of morbid amusement. M. de Baschi, who was Madame de Pompadour's brother-in-law and French ambassador to Portugal, lived through the quake and, upon his return to Versailles, entertained the court with his eyewitness testimony. Evidently Baschi's account of the demise of the Spanish ambassador, the Conde de Perelada, had his audience in stitches; as fate would have it, Perelada was crushed by the coat-of-arms of Spain, which crowned the portico of his embassy, as he tried to escape during the earthquake. In truth, Louis XV had instructed his ambassador to Lisbon to inform the Portuguese of his disposition to help, but nothing ever came of the indifferent offer. Nor did the Netherlands prove to be charitable, although for wholly different reasons. To the stern Dutch Calvinist clergy, the Lisbon earthquake was a just response of the living God to Portugal's penchant for superstition, idol worship, and popery. Accordingly, the States General of the United Provinces of the Free Netherlands sent nothing.

Still, the aid that Portugal did receive from abroad was considerable and thoroughly unprecedented. Never had a natural disaster inspired an outpouring of international aid, neither the Great

London Fire of 1666, for example, nor the calamitous flood that virtually drowned the Netherlands in 1565. For reasons of national pride and a jealous sense of sovereignty, the notion of foreign relief would previously have been unthinkable. By 1755, however, military and political alliances, mutual commercial interests, and improvements in travel and communications had made the states of Europe increasingly interdependent, and the Lisbon earthquake struck a chord of collective, although not universal, compassion. No one was more surprised by the response than the Portuguese. Just before Christmas, Abraham Castres brought word of the British largesse to King José I and Queen Maria Ana, still camped out at Belém. "Their looks and tone of voice plainly showed the emotion of their hearts," Castres wrote, "and how sensibly they were touched with this most signal mark of His Majesty's attention to and compassion for the distress of their subjects." After the royal audience Castres found himself surrounded by nobles and courtiers who expressed "their most agreeable surprise, upon knowing that I had not been charged with empty compliments only, but also with such proofs of real grandeur and dignity as would confer eternal honour both upon our gracious sovereign, and the whole British nation. Many warm declarations of this kind I met with from people of all ranks."[12]

The British relief ships, setting sail from Portsmouth and Dublin (the food stores were mostly Irish), were delayed for months due to rough seas and contrary winds, but when they finally did reach Lisbon, Carvalho insisted that the city's British residents be the first to benefit from the relief. "Dispositions are actually making for the distribution of the beef and butter among the poor," reported Castres, "but this court has insisted upon ours being the first served, which, M. Carvalho says, was a step they were obliged to, out of gratitude as well as decency."[13]

CHAPTER THREE

TAKING STOCK

I can not say for certain how many people died on this construction [the stone quay], as I am waiting for a good swimmer from Angola, so that I can send him down there, even though it may be a bit expensive, to know if I can count on three or four hundred, and then I'll tell you for certain.

—José Acúrsio de Tavares, February 1756

No amount of gracious aid or genuine compassion could make up for what Lisbon had irretrievably lost. The human casualties alone were immense and largely incalculable. Records of births and deaths might have provided a fairly accurate census, but fire had consumed many parish church archives. Neither could there be a proper accounting of those who had taken flight from the city and never returned, or many of the victims of the tsunamis who were simply washed away, or those reduced to ashes by the fire. The death toll swelled, as many of the severely injured failed to recover from their wounds. Just how many people were lost in the disaster has long been a subject of debate, and any precise reckoning is virtually impossible to verify. The original estimates in the immediate aftermath of the earthquake placed the death toll at close to 100,000, nearly half the city's population, but that figure was soon refuted by contemporary sources as wildly inflated. Probably a quarter as many lost their lives, although some observers such as Father Manuel Portal insisted that "in the opinion of prudent and learned people who are not influenced by the voice of the populace, the number will be between twelve and fifteen thousand."[1]

But even the moderate estimates of tens of thousands of victims are chilling enough. In a matter of days Lisbon lost roughly

10 percent of its 250,000 inhabitants; the city was quite literally decimated. And while a considerable proportion of the dead were Lisbon's poor, whose insubstantial hovels least resisted the shocks, the earthquake was by nature wholly indiscriminate. Among the city's sizable religious community, 204 were killed, including 63 nuns from the order of Santa Clara, whose church and convent were utterly leveled. Those who were faithfully attending mass were perhaps the worst hit. Six hundred were buried beneath the ruins in the Franciscan convent; 400 were lost in the Santa Trindade Church; 300 were crushed in the Convent of Nossa Senhora da Penha de França; and 137 were burned to death in the Sé Cathedral. They all had the consolation of expiring on sanctified ground.

Only a handful of the victims came from the city's noble ranks, but among them were Maria da Graça de Castro, Marquesa de Louriçal, and Manuel Varejão de Távora, Inquisitor of Lisbon, both of whom came from two of the country's most prominent aristocratic families.* The minister of finance perished, and so too did the secretary of war. Especially tragic was the death by fire of the 400 inmates in the Hospital de Todos os Santos. Of the 67 British subjects who lost their lives, including 49 women, Abraham Castres saw fit to distinguish between the victims: "Of the British and Irish nations together, though the latter were extremely numerous, particularly as to the poorer sort, I do not hear of above sixty missing, most of whom are so obscure as not to be known to any but the Irish friars."[2] Clearly some deaths were mourned more acutely than others. Giles Vincent, a merchant and member of the British Factory, was

---

*The low casualty figures among the nobles can be explained, at least in part, by the fact that most attended mass in their private chapels, usually at the comfortable hour of eleven o'clock. Sheltered in substantial palaces, they avoided getting caught in the street or among the throng when the quake struck.

eulogized with a poem entitled "Occasioned by the Death of Mr. G. Vincent, in the late most dreadful Calamity at Lisbon," which was published in *The Gentleman's Magazine* in February 1813:

Unhappy youth! what sin can be thy crime?
Thus to be taken in thy very prime,
From parents, friends,—who now incessant mourn
Thy cruel fate—by death relentless torn.
But let us not presume the ways of God to scan,
Whose works are always just—the cause tho' hid from man.[3]

A smattering of other foreign residents and visitors, among them Germans, Dutch, Spaniards (including the ambassador), and Italians, also met their deaths in Lisbon. Roundly overlooked by the common census and the history books were the untold scores of African slaves who perished in the Cadeia da Galé prison and in the houses and palaces of their masters. Eighty-odd criminals and thieves were summarily hung high from the gallows, but they were victims not so much of the earthquake as of their own avarice and appetites.

Lisbon's material destruction had no precedents in European history: neither the burning of Rome or London nor the sacking of Carthage or Constantinople, to name but a few paradigms of ruin, approached the totality of the cataclysm. Only the snuffing-out of Pompeii was commensurate in violence, but that event was impossibly distant in time and indeterminate in place.* Not sur-

---

*Thanks to Pliny the Younger, a detailed description of the eruption of Vesuvius and the destruction of Pompeii was well known. But not until 1763, when archaeologists digging in the shadows of the volcano uncovered an inscription with the words *Res Publica Pompeianorum,* was the actual site of ancient Pompeii definitively determined.

prisingly then, it was to biblical ruin that the contemporaries of the Lisbon earthquake invariably referred when attempting to conjure up the scale of the destruction. Lisbon was likened variably to Jericho, Babylon, Nineveh, and Sodom and Gomorrah.

Alas, the area of Lisbon worst hit by both the earthquake and the fire was also the city's most populous and prosperous, home to its most important political, economic, ecclesiastical, and commercial institutions. The area extended from Castle Hill in the east to the Rua do Século in the west, and from the Tagus shore to a point roughly one mile inland. Within this nucleus lay the Paço da Ribeira waterfront palace, the Customs Exchange, government offices, the public tribunals, the Casa da India, the Mint, the Sé Cathedral, dozens of churches and convents, the central market, the Ribeira das Naus shipyard, the new Opera House, the headquarters of the Inquisition, the Hospital de Todos os Santos, the Terreiro do Paço and Rossio squares, and the entire Baixa quarter, where the lion's share of Lisbon's merchants and traders had their shops and warehouses. Of these structures, only the Mint survived unscathed. In one blow the city had lost its ability to govern, to conduct commerce, to worship in its churches, and to communicate—in short, to function.

Had the fire not occurred, or had the flames been at least partially contained, much might have been recovered from the ruins; as it was, the conflagration did more irreparable damage than the quake itself. In the immediate aftermath of the quake scores of merchants in the Baixa quarter dug through the heaps of rubble that were their former shops and emporiums and managed to salvage a portion of their wares, only to see them consumed by the subsequent fire. Up in smoke too went innumerable accounts and ledgers, commercial documents, and letters of credit on which the merchants' livelihoods depended. "Most of the merchants are

absolutely ruined; there are two houses that have lost 50,000 l.
[pounds] each, none of them know who are their debtors, their
books of accounts having been consumed in the flames, and if
they had saved them, to what purpose, the inhabitants in general
becoming insolvent under this misfortune," wrote one understandably anxious British merchant.[4] In the Customs Exchange
and waterfront warehouses, stores of gold, diamonds, jasper, sugar,
tobacco, cacao, hides, cotton, silk, exotic woods, and a catalog of
other valuable commodities were either ruined, washed away by
the tsunamis, or engulfed by the flames.

Neither Lisbon nor even Portugal as a whole bore the loss
alone. At the time of the quake Lisbon was a port of the first rank
for both intra-European and global trade with the Americas, Africa, and Asia, and what transpired in the Portuguese capital affected, among others and to varying degrees, Brazilian farmers
and miners, Asian spice producers, Indian silk manufacturers,
British wool producers, French tanners, Hamburg timber merchants, Dutch tobacconists, Jewish diamond cutters in Antwerp
and Amsterdam, and even colonial American fishermen. In a letter to Boston merchants dated November 6, which appeared in
the *Pennsylvania Gazette* on January 8, 1756, a British trader sta-
tioned in Lisbon spelled out the loss on a shipment of dried cod,
or *bacalhau*, a frequent commodity, along with cotton, tobacco,
and timber, in the trade between the American colonies and
Portugal:

I have not Time, nor am in a Capacity to expatiate
on this Affair, I must therefore refer you to Captain
Collins for the Particular. Let it suffice to inform you,
That I sold your Fish; but alas! It is all lost and destroyed in the universal Catastrophe: I have heard

nothing of the Buyer since the Disaster; and greatly doubtful whether he will be in a Capacity to pay. In short, we are all like to lose our outstanding Debts . . . I shall stay in this miserable Place for the Sake of my Friends, and will endeavour all in my Power to save what I can of your Effects.

There were an untold number of similar reports of economic loss and ruin; and strangely, some accounts even allowed for a supernatural flourish. In a lengthy missive dated November 18 an anonymous British merchant in Lisbon mentions to a London colleague the peculiar case of a German trader whose disregard for the veracity of dreams reads like a cautionary tale for the paranormal:

One Mr. Burmester, a Hamburgh Merchant of this place, had received a letter from his partner at Hamburgh, advising him to remove a large quantity of flax, and other valuable effects, from the house he then resided in, to several distant ware-houses in different parts of the City, giving as a reason for his desiring him to use this precaution, that he had dreamed for 14 nights together, that the City of Lisbon was all on fire. You may depend on the veracity of this fact as here related, since Mr. Burmester publickly showed his letter to every body. But whether the advice was owing to any supernatural warning, or merely, accidental 'twas of no matter of signification, as he did not pay the least regard to it, so that his goods shared the same fate, with the rest of his neighbours.[5]

All told, the scale of the commercial and financial disaster was astronomical. British merchants alone lost an estimated seven million pounds sterling in goods; the Hamburg merchants suffered to the order of two million pounds; the Portuguese losses were well-nigh impossible to calculate.

As severe as the economic losses were, in time business would inevitably resume. By contrast, there was no way to recuperate the inestimable wealth of books, manuscripts, paintings, sculpture, tapestries, furniture, and objets d'art that had filled Lisbon's royal and privates palaces and helped to stoke the fire. At the palace of the Marquês de Louriçal, one of the first places where fire broke out following the quake, a magnificent collection of more than two hundred paintings, including works by Titian, Correggio, and Rubens, were reduced to ashes, along with a library of eighty thousand books, one thousand manuscripts (not least of which was a history by Emperor Charles V written in his own hand), and a priceless collection of maps, charts, and commentaries by the great Portuguese explorers in their voyages of discovery in Africa, Asia, and the New World. The royal library, in which King João V had accumulated seventy thousand volumes (including the Hebrew bibles and religious texts that Carvalho had acquired in London), was lost in the fire that gutted the riverside palace. Other important libraries burned at the convents of São Domingos, Carmo, São Francisco, Trindade, and Boa-Hora. The accumulated stocks of thirty booksellers were likewise consumed. Sadly, there was no recompense for the loss of this sort of cultural patrimony; the disaster stripped Portugal of a legacy that the country would never recover.

As if by a miracle, a number of conspicuous edifices and resources weathered the triple assault of earthquake, tsunami, and fire. Located on the Rua São Paulo, just north of the shipyard, the Mint was one of the few buildings in the central district to remain standing. That it survived intact was a particular blessing (and a thorny issue for the preachers who claimed that God was chastising Lisbon for, among other sins, a lust for gold). More astonishing was the fact that the kingdom's abundant store of gold was not consummately looted by the mob, but for this beneficence king and country had a mere boy to thank. It is one of those extraordinary incidents that sometimes inexplicably arise in a catastrophe; the details emerged in an anonymous letter, now in the archives of the British Historical Society of Portugal. In the midst of the disaster an Englishman stood alone and stranded by the riverside, having barely escaped his collapsing house and the fury of the tsunamis.

I was now in such a situation that I knew not which way to turn myself. If I remained there, I was in danger from the sea; if I retired farther from the shore the houses threatened certain destruction. At last I resolved to go to the Mint, which being a low and very strong building, had met with no considerable damage except in some of the apartments toward the river. The party of soldiers, which is every day set here on guard, had all deserted the place, and the only person that remained was the commanding officer, a nobleman's son about 17 or 18 years of age, whom I found standing at the gate. As there was still a continual tremor of the earth, and the place where we now stood, being within 20 or 30 feet of the opposite houses, (which were all tottering) appeared too dangerous and the court yard was full of water, we both retired inwards to an hillock of stones and rubbish. Here I entered into conversation with him and having expressed my admiration, that one so young should have had the courage to keep his post when everyone of his soldiers had deserted theirs, the answer he made was: "that tho' he were sure, the earth should open, and swallow him up, he scorned to think of flying from his post." In short 'twas owing to the magnanimity of this young Gentleman, that the Mint, which at this time had upwards of two Millions of money in it, was not robbed, and indeed I do him no more than justice in saying that I never saw anyone behave with equal serenity and composure, on occasions much less dreadful than the present.[6]

The young officer was Lieutenant Bartolomeu de Sousa Mexia, and his valor went neither unnoticed nor unrewarded. Shortly after the disaster the resolute lieutenant was summoned to Belém, where King José I promoted him to the rank of captain. It is unclear whether the new captain also received a token measure of what he had so steadfastly defended.

Two million pieces of gold was no small bounty, and foreign aid apart, it would prove essential to the relief of the survivors, the maintenance of the government apparatus, and the eventual rebuilding of Lisbon. Had it not been for the preservation of the Mint, Lisbon would have been not only broken down but virtually broke, at least temporarily. Portugal's dependence on its Brazilian gold and diamond mines was nearly total, and in the absence of an effective industrial and agricultural base, gold and gems paid for a host of essential imports, including wheat, cloth, and, almost unpardonably for a maritime nation, fish. Replenishing the royal coffers would have taken months if not years. Still, that with all that the city had lost only the Mint survived was a cruel irony, for all the gold in the realm could not erase the only deficit that would haunt Lisbon for generations, that of lives. The paradox was not lost on the preachers, who quickly took to quoting the book of Zephaniah: "Neither their silver nor their gold shall be able to deliver them on the day of the wrath of the Lord." Perhaps not, but the gold stores did much indisputable good to succor a beaten populace and to restore a city that many observers, most notably the clergy, regarded as irredeemable.

For all the destruction that the tsunamis wreaked on the Tagus, it was principally smaller vessels that were sunk or battered against the shore. The Portuguese men-of-war and frigates, including those of the Brazilian fleet, that had dropped anchor in Lisbon only days before the disaster rode out the waves with little or no damage. The survival of the fleet was all the more important since the Ribeira das Naus shipyard was utterly destroyed and no new ships could be commissioned in the foreseeable future. Without its fleet, Lisbon would have been at the mercy of Barbary pirates, cut off from international communication and its lucrative colonies, and deprived of the trade that was the city's lifeblood.

Lisbon also preserved another vital element, fresh water. The monumental thirty-six-mile Aqueduto das Águas Livres, commissioned by João V and inaugurated in 1748, conveyed water to Lisbon from the northeast and alleviated a centuries-old problem of periodic drought. Designed by the military engineers Manuel da Maia, Custódio Vieira, and Carlos Mardel, the structure included an expansive viaduct of thirty-five arches, at points exceeding two hundred feet in height, and became a civil engineering marvel of the day. Rather inexplicably, the aqueduct withstood the quake, and the water was used to help fight the fire (although the effort was mostly futile) and to slake the thirst of the survivors. A lack of fresh water would have led to epidemics and the swelling of the already prodigious death toll.

All of Portugal could also rejoice in the survival of the king and the entire royal family, who came through the ordeal, as it were, without a scratch. In the intensely hierarchical scheme of an absolute monarchy, the king was paterfamilias and protector, a divinely endowed embodiment of the nation whose demise would have spelled a sense of hopelessness among his subjects and likely touched off a complicated if not violent struggle for succession. The message that the king was alive and well was interpreted by survivors as a sign of promise and a guarantee that they would not be further forsaken. Call it the result of providence, a twist of fate, or sheer unmitigated luck, but the early morning outing to Belém on All Saints' saved the whole royal lot and their considerable entourage. One look at the riverside palace, toppled by the quake and swept by the fire, was enough to convince anyone that the royal family would have had little hope of survival had they been in residence. The deliverance of the monarch (and of Carvalho, who acted in his name) signified the preservation of authority; without him the pillage and murderous chaos in the immediate wake of the disaster might well have become a pandemic. Furthermore, it was to José I that international aid was delivered for the solace of *his* subjects; indeed, no other institution but the Crown was in a position to properly administer and dispense the relief. And last, the king's salvation and that of his family also helped to uphold Portuguese independence, as a formidable anti-Portuguese faction in the Spanish court in Madrid was only too eager for a pretext to recover what had been, albeit briefly, Spain's westernmost territory.*

---

*From 1580 to 1640, a period that came to be known as the "Babylonian Captivity," Spain, under Felipe II, did indeed annex Portugal. The Spanish Habsburg king was alleged to have said of Portugal: "I inherited it, I bought it, and I conquered it."

Gold to confront the recovery, ships to defend the coast and maintain channels of communication, a king to lead, and water to drink—these were hardly insignificant blessings under the circumstances. But the catastrophe had laid waste a city whose origins stretched back to the Phoenicians. Throughout its eight-hundred-year history Lisbon had succumbed to Visigoth, Moorish, and Castilian invaders; it had been besieged, visited by the Black Death, and annexed by its more powerful Iberian neighbor. The order of destruction caused by the earthquake, however, was ineffable, as close to a veritable hell as an earthly calamity could come. Allusions to the Apocalypse were not far off the mark; indeed, they were the only references that captured the singular scale of the horror. An English survivor signed off a letter from the devastated city with the phrase "from the Place which *was*, but *is not* Lisbon." It was true. No traveler returning to the city would have recognized the place; the hills would be there, of course, and the Tagus, and the odd edifice that withstood the upheaval, but Lisbon was no more. The old city would survive only in the memory of a generation that could still conjure up fleeting images of medieval lanes and former palaces, of cityscapes and vistas that conformed to the old geography, and of the countenances of victims before the Fall. But in time those too would perish, and the Lisbon of old would vanish forever with scarcely a trace. "Who has not seen Lisbon has not lived" went an old dictum whose logic no longer held.

CHAPTER FOUR

ALIS UBBO ... OLISIPO ... AL-USHBUNA ... LISBOA

This city did indeed, as I believe, once belong to your people, but now it is ours. In the future it will perhaps be yours. But this shall be in accordance with divine favour. While God willed we have held it; when he shall have willed otherwise, we shall no longer hold it.

—Osbernus, *De expugnatione Lyxbonensi,* 1147

L isboans had believed their city to be eternal, or at least im-
memorial. The origins of the city were indeed ancient and
obscure, but the persistent claim that Ulysses had founded the
port after the sack of Troy—hence Lisbon's ancient title of
Olisipo—is wholly apocryphal. The etymological root comes,
more probably, from the Phoenicians, who called the place Alis
Ubbo, or "Friendly Bay." Greeks and Carthaginians followed
the Phoenicians, but it was the Romans, sweeping into western
Iberia in the second century B.C. and defeating the local Lusita-
nian tribes, who left antiquity's most pronounced mark on Lisbon. The Romans saw at once the strategic importance and
aesthetic appeal of Olisipo's expansive harbor on the northern
shore of the Tagus in proximity to the Atlantic. What was more,
the land was verdant and fertile and the climate equable; and the
Lusitani, although initially fiercely resistant to the Roman invaders, soon grasped the social, economic, and intellectual advantages of Romanization. Olisipo was elevated to the status of a
municipium, and Julius Caesar gave it the sonorous epithet *Felici-
tas Julia*, that is, "the Happiness of Julio." Lusitania, as the Romans
called western Iberia, provided Rome with salt, grains, dried fish,
marble, minerals, and much-prized horses. In return, the locals

reaped the fruits bestowed by Rome, including Roman law, Roman administration and fiscal practices, Roman public works from roads to baths to aqueducts, a pantheon of Roman gods, and Roman art and literature—in a word, civilization.

Nearly half a millennium of peace and prosperity was snuffed out in Lusitania, as elsewhere in the Roman Empire, by the Germanic invasions. The Suevi descended on Lusitania in the fourth century, and the Visigoths followed two hundred years later, but compared to the profound impact left by Rome, the legacy of these northern "barbarians" was negligible save for a more militant notion of Christianity. Under Roman rule early Christian evangelists had reached Iberia and preached the new creed, but the Germanic invaders gave the faith official sanction, giving rise to the church that would become the most enduring institution in Portuguese history.

The Cross, however, was soon eclipsed by the Crescent Moon. To the Muslim armies and their Berber camp followers who overran Iberia in the early eighth century, Lusitania was known simply as al-Gharb, "the West." The new masters made Lisbon, or Lishbuna, or al-Ushbuna, as they called the town, a citadel, built the colossal fortress that would later go by the Christian denomination of Castelo de São Jorge, and transformed the old Roman temples into mosques. It was the start of five hundred years of Islamic high culture in Portugal. Henceforth the days of Lishbuna were punctuated by the calls to prayer of the muezzin.

All of Europe shuddered at the arrival of Muslim invaders on the Continent, even if it was in far-off Iberia, but the newcomers proved to be remarkably mild overlords, and their rule was marked less by religious zeal than by sheer practicality. During the Visigoths' rule Lisbon's Jews had suffered relentless persecution, but under the Muslims both Christian and Jewish religious practices were openly tolerated. As long as the locals professed allegiance to the Caliphate, which ruled from Damascus, and paid their poll tax (from which children, the elderly, cripples, and the financially destitute were mercifully exempt), the new masters seemed not only willing but eager to leave religion out of the picture.

That the Muslims, especially the Arabs who made up the ruling elite, were the intellectual betters of their Christian subjects is hardly surprising given the centuries of benighted Gothic rule in Iberia. They ushered in a scientific and cultural awakening at a time when western Europe was still hopelessly mired in the Dark Ages. It was through the Arabic translations of Plato, Hippocrates, Galen, and above all Aristotle, for example, that Europe rediscovered the Greek classics that had all but disappeared in the West, victims of an early Christian book-burning craze that sought to extinguish any flame associated with the pagan past. The Arabs brought knowledge of astronomy, cartography, navigation (including the introduction of the astrolabe and the compass), and shipbuilding, which would give the Portuguese a distinct advantage in their own Age of Discovery in the fifteenth and sixteenth centuries. The advances in agriculture were no less groundbreaking and helped ease the dreary lot of the serfs who comprised the majority of the local population. The old system of Roman irrigation was vastly improved; crop rotations, fruit orchards, rice paddies, and mechanized corn milling were introduced. Al-Gharb blossomed.

Lisbon, like Seville, Valencia, Granada, and Córdoba (the capital of Moorish Iberia), took on a thoroughly oriental air. Palaces went up, and a casbahlike neighborhood arose on the eastern side of the city where hot springs (*alhama*) had been discovered.* Public baths were opened, gardens laid out, and fountains built.

---

*Today Lisbon's Alfama remains one of the city's quintessential quarters.

Luminous glazed tiles, or *azuleif*, were introduced as a decorative motif. Although the lingua franca among the locals in the streets was still a Latinized dialect, Arabic was the language of the rulers, and an Arabic scientific and technical vocabulary was adopted in architecture, shipbuilding, and navigation. Penning Arabic verse became a favorite diversion of the learned. Given the manifest sophistication and urbanity of the Arabs, a goodly portion of the local population, whose tradition of Christian faith was only centuries old and tepid at best, converted to the new religion that seemed to herald a bright and prosperous future. Conversion instantly enveloped the Muslim initiates into a vast Islamic brotherhood with global ambitions. Christianity, by contrast, looked increasingly like a thing of the past.

Christianity may have been dormant during the Muslim occupation, but it was far from spent. In the mountains of northern Portugal a tenacious Christian faith weathered Islamization, and here the vanguard of the Reconquest gathered strength and resources to begin the campaign to expel the Muslims. During the eleventh century these northern Christians, reinforced by bands of mercenary French knights and their ragtag followers, were making increasingly bold forays south into the Muslim-held territories. A Christian enclave emerged around Oporto, which became known as Portucalia, a name derived from the ancient port of Portus Cale. In the twelfth century Afonso Henriques, a Burgundian count at the head of the Christian forces, proclaimed himself king of Portugal, and the struggle with the Moors, exacerbated by the increasingly harsh rule of the North African Almoravid dynasty, took on the fervor of a full-blown western crusade. In battle the tide turned in favor of the Christians, and in 1147 Afonso and his army of the Cross were camped outside the Muslim walls of Lisbon, readying for a siege.

As it happened, some entirely fortuitous support had washed up on Afonso's shore. In the spring of 1147 a fleet of some two hundred ships, carrying English, Frankish, Frisian, Norman, Scottish, and Flemish Crusaders, had set sail from Dartmouth, England, bound for the ill-fated Second Crusade. Storms blew the fleet off course, and the ships sought shelter in Oporto, where the local bishop convinced the Crusaders (or simply "the Franks," as they were referred to in chronicles) to continue on to Lisbon and join Afonso in his attack on the Muslim citadel. The Crusader ranks were divided over the wisdom of diverting from their sworn mission—to aid the embattled Latin kingdom in the Holy Land—in order to liberate an Iberian city from the Moors, but the Portuguese bishops relieved their Christian consciences by assuring them that smiting Muslims in Lisbon offered the same spiritual rewards as doing so in Antioch, Tripoli, Edessa, or Jerusalem. And, of course, there was the booty to consider. Lisbon was a prosperous Muslim port, a city of some sixty thousand families, and within its well-fortified walls lay much to plunder. At the Crusaders' first meeting with Afonso outside Lisbon in June, the king tried to persuade them to fight for the exclusive benefit of the faith. The Crusaders balked and threatened to abandon the enterprise, but when the king promised loot, titles, and land to the victors, they agreed to join the battle:

> Let the covenant of agreement between me and the Franks be known to all the sons of the church, both present and to come. To wit, that I Affonso, king of the Portuguese . . . grant by this charter of confirmation that the Franks who are about to remain with me at the siege of the city of Lisbon may take into their own power and possession, and may keep, all the

possessions of the enemy myself and all my men having absolutely no share in them. If any shall wish to
have enemy captives redeemed alive, they shall freely
have the ransom money, and they shall turn the said
captives over to me. If perchance they should take the
city, they shall have it and hold it until it has been
searched and despoiled, both through putting everyone to ransom and otherwise. And so, at last, after it
has been ransacked to their full satisfaction, they shall
hand it over to me.[1]

Before the siege began in earnest, the Christian forces were
compelled by Afonso to attempt a last-ditch effort at diplomacy. A
party of Christian negotiators led by John, the archbishop of Braga,
was sent to parley with the Muslim *alcayde,* or governor, the local
Mozarabic bishop, and a group of Lishbuna city fathers who had
gathered on the battlement to hear the Christian offer. An account of this momentous Christian-Muslim exchange was recorded
by an English priest in the Crusader ranks named Osbern of Bawdsey, or Osbernus, in his *De expugnatione Lyxbonensi* (*The Conquest
of Lisbon*). After some preliminary words of harmony and concord,
the archbishop came to the Christian point:

We demand that the see of this city shall be under
our law; and surely, if a natural sense of justice had
made any progress among you, you would go back un-
bidden to the land of the Moors from whence you
came, with your baggage, money, and goods, and your
women and children, leaving to us our own. However,
we already know full well that you would only do such
a thing unwillingly and as a result of force. But consider

a voluntary departure; for, if you yield willingly to our demands, you have already escaped the bitterest part of them. For how otherwise there could be peace between us I know not, since the lot assigned to each from the beginning lacks its rightful possessor. You Moors and Moabites fraudulently seized the realm of Lusitania from your king and ours. From then until now there has been desolation in cities, villages, and churches without number, and it still goes on. On the one side in this struggle your fealty, on the other human society itself, has been violated.[2]

The archbishop then proceeded to expound on Lisbon's Christian heritage; he quoted Saint James the Apostle, who first brought the Gospel to Iberia; he rattled off the names of the early Christian martyrs who had died for their faith under the Romans; he recalled illustrious ecclesiastics and great Church councils. Then once again he kindly but unequivocally asked the Muslim usurpers to, in a phrase, get out of town. From the Muslim perspective high up on the battlement, the Christian plea must have come across as at once brash and slightly ridiculous. The Moors, after all, were exceedingly well entrenched inside Lisbon's fortified walls. They considered themselves not temporary invaders but settled masters, having occupied the city for some four centuries; nor did they have any intention of returning to sun-scorched North Africa. One of the men in the Muslim party stepped forward to respond to the archbishop:

Not yet have we decided to hand over our city unconditionally to you or to remain in it and become your subjects. Not yet has our magnanimity advanced

to the point where we would give up certainties for
uncertainties. For in large affairs decisions must be
made with largeness of view. This city did indeed, as I
believe, once belong to your people, but now it is ours.
In the future it will perhaps be yours. But this shall be
in accordance with divine favour. While God willed
we have held it; when he shall have willed otherwise,
we shall no longer hold it. For there is no wall which
is impregnable against the arbitrament of his will.
Therefore, let us be content with whatsoever shall
please God, who has so often saved our blood from
your hands . . . But get you hence, for entry into the
city lies not open to you except through trial of sword.
For your threats and the tumults of barbarians, whose
strength we know better than their language, are not
highly valued among us.[3]

The siege began on July 1, 1147. The Christian forces, by now
well versed in the military art of besieging Muslims in their fortified strongholds, attacked the walls of Lisbon with catapults, rams,
siege towers, and teams of sappers, hoping to create a breach
through which the fifteen-thousand-strong Christian army could
penetrate the city. The Muslim defenders, however, proved remarkably resilient, and Lisbon held out for a full seventeen weeks.
But by October its inhabitants were starving to death, and the
stench from the accumulating corpses inside the city walls had
grown vile. Lisbon was falling. In October the Muslims brokered
a truce and agreed to surrender the city to King Afonso, provided
that the garrison and the inhabitants be allowed to retreat un-
harmed. The king entered Lisbon with a contingent of Anglo-
Norman, Flemish, and German Crusaders on October 24, raised

the Christian ensign—a red cross on a white field—from the highest tower of the Muslim citadel, and gathered the clergy and the people to intone the *Te Deum laudamus*. Then the rapine began. Osbern of Bawdsey lays the blame for the patently un-Christian behavior squarely on the Flemish and Germans in the Crusader camp: "the men of Cologne and the Flemings, when they saw so many temptations to greed in the city, observed not the bond of their oath or plighted faith. They rushed about hither and thither, they pillaged; they broke open doors; they tore open the innermost parts of every house; they drove out the citizens and treated them with insults, against right and justice; they scattered utensils and clothing; they insulted maidens; they made wrong equal with right; they secretly snatched away all those things which ought to have been made the common property of all the forces. They even slew the aged bishop of the city, against all right and decency, by cutting his throat."[4]

Despite the cold-blooded and unwarranted murder of the Mozarabic bishop, whom the Crusaders seem to have taken for a Moorish collaborator, the fall of Lisbon did not degenerate into indiscriminate bloodletting. The city was most thoroughly sacked, it's true, but the Muslim garrison, along with a legion of Muslim residents who opted to quit Lisbon rather than live under Christian-barbarian rule, were allowed to depart peacefully, if virtually empty-handed. According to Osbern, the vanquished left the city through three gates continuously from Saturday morning until the following Wednesday: "There was such a multitude of people that it seemed as if all of Spain were mingled in the crowd."

Henceforth Lisbon would stand as a shining example to Christendom of a city retaken and redeemed by the Cross, and the new rulers lost little time in re-Christianizing the place. The city's principal mosque was razed in a fit of zealotry aimed at exorcising

the infidel, and in its place the Sé Cathedral was built to commemorate the Reconquest. Gilbert of Hastings, one of the English Crusaders, was elected Lisbon's new bishop. As the shifting
circumstances seemed to dictate, many locals prudently converted
back to Christianity; those who remained firm in their Islamic
faith mostly retreated with their Muslim lords and brethren south
to the Algarve, to Andalusia, or back across the strait to North
Africa—"the land of the Moors from whence they came"—as the
archbishop of Braga had so bluntly recommended. As for the Crusaders, they continued on their journey to the Holy Land, where
they joined in the costly and futile siege of Damascus and eventually limped home in defeat. Indeed, the whole enterprise of the
Second Crusade was an unmitigated failure with the exception of
the conquest of Lisbon. The Moors would attempt repeatedly to
retake their beloved al-Ushbuna but would be repulsed. By the
middle of the thirteenth century the Christian forces had battled
their way south and expelled the Muslim armies from their last
stronghold in the "Kingdom of the West" in the Algarve, ending
nearly five hundred years of Muslim rule.

Naturally Christian Europe rejoiced, but religious convictions
aside, the average Portuguese had little to celebrate. The Moors
may well have been conquerors, usurpers, and the minions of a
distant caliph, but they left Portugal far better off than they had
found it, and after their departure, much of what they had nurtured was squandered. Agricultural lands that the Muslims had
scientifically cultivated were mismanaged or abandoned by the
Christians; Lisbon's place in the great Muslim commercial empire
that stretched from the Indian Ocean to Iberia was suddenly lost;
and Arabic culture was abruptly extinguished. The few Muslims
who remained after the conquest found themselves reduced to
the status of second-class citizens or, worse, enslaved and forced

to live in a Muslim ghetto that became known as the Mouraria, "the place of the Moors," located beneath the ramparts of the citadel. The Alfama, once an exclusive Moorish neighborhood, was given over to Christian artisans and fishermen.

If the Christian inclinations of the Portuguese had formerly been halfhearted, the Western Crusades and the Reconquest spawned a more stalwart faith, a faith forged by the sword and sustained by the Cross, that would mark the country's religious character for centuries. This newfound Christian conviction was not the cause but rather the consequence of the Reconquest. The Catholic Church filled the vacuum left by the expulsion of the Moors, granting vast tracts of land for settlement to religious orders such as the Cistercians and the marauding Knights Templar. Along with a nascent monarchy, the Church became the foundation on which Portugal rose as a nation. The country owed its very existence to the Crusades, and it would never quite shed either its Crusader sense of mission or the religious intolerance that it bred.

Having long succumbed to myriad conquerors—Romans, Suevi, Visigoths, and Moors—Portugal embarked on a slew of conquests of its own. The Age of Discovery, or perhaps more properly the Age of Exploitation, dawned in 1415 when a Portuguese military force led by Prince Henrique of Aviz, the son of King João I, crossed the Strait of Gibraltar and captured the Moroccan city of Ceuta. The victory was more than just a footnote in the long-running Christian-Muslim saga; it marked an epochal shift in European consciousness in which the introspection and detachment that characterized much of medieval Europe (the Crusades notwithstanding) came abruptly to an end. Suddenly there was an unplumbed world to discover, untold riches to acquire, and fabulous lands to claim and conquer, and it was

Portugal, on the fringe of the known world and hitherto largely inconsequential on the European stage, that led the way.

The impetus behind many, although not all, of the initial voyages of discovery was provided by Prince Henrique, known to the Portuguese as O Infante Dom Henrique and to history as Prince Henry the Navigator. The son of King João I and Philippa of Lancaster, Prince Henry has long assumed mythic proportions in the popular imagination of the Portuguese. In an age of exploration to uncharted waters, where savage races and fantastical beasts were said to reside, the exploits of the prince and scores of other heroic navigators, adventurers, and mariners became the stuff of national legend. In truth, Henry never ventured beyond Morocco, but he did extend patronage to dozens of expeditions through the auspices of the knightly Order of Christ, of which he was head. Little about these historic voyages was even remotely Christian; for Prince Henry and every other explorer, the only motive worth risking one's life for was a handsome profit. It had been the prince's intention upon invading Morocco to oust the Moors and thus control the North African plains, once the breadbasket of Rome, but when his Christian forces were unable to advance beyond Ceuta, he turned his attention to the Atlantic and the western coast of Africa.

On the sea, Portugal's lateen-rigged caravels were the fastest and most maneuverable vessels afloat, and it wasn't long before they were reaching uncharted waters. Madeira, the Azores, and the Canary Islands were the first modest ultramarine conquests to be planted with the Portuguese flag, and they were cultivated for traditional crops such as wheat, wine, sugar, and timber. But as the Portuguese ships ventured farther south, exploring the West African coast, their captains and crews discovered two commodities that would become staples in Portugal's economic development and forever change both the face and the fortunes of the nation: slaves and gold. For centuries Europe had known that gold was transported from the African interior by Moroccan caravans bound for the great ports of the Maghreb, but by going directly to the source and shipping the gold to Europe by sea, Portugal effectively cut out the middlemen and achieved an unstinting monopoly on West African gold. The Portuguese settlement on Africa's Gold Coast (present-day Ghana) was christened, aptly, São Jorge da Mina, or Saint George of the Mine, and by the late fifteenth century the gold trade was filling the royal coffers in Lisbon (it was a monopoly of the Crown) with roughly half a ton of bullion a year.

Slaving was scarcely less rewarding. The profit on a healthy Mauretanian slave was estimated at 700 percent, the kind of margin that induced ordinary merchant seamen to become ferocious slavers almost overnight. Soon the trade in human commodity was booming, thanks to general cupidity and the Church's official sanction. Nothing spurred the slave trade quite so effectively as Pope Nicholas V's papal bull *Romanus Pontifex* of 1455, which granted Portugal the right "to invade, search out, capture, vanquish, and subdue all Saracens and pagans whatsoever, and other enemies of Christ wheresoever placed, and the kingdoms, dukedoms, principalities, dominions, possessions, and all movable and immovable goods whatsoever held and possessed by them and to reduce their persons to perpetual slavery, and to apply and appropriate to himself and his successors the kingdoms, dukedoms, counties, principalities, dominions, possessions, and goods, and to convert them to his and their use and profit." What made the whole exploit especially nefarious was the brute commercial logic with which it was pursued.

Contrary to popular belief, the Portuguese did not conduct raids into the African interior to kidnap the natives; they didn't have to. Rather, they procured slaves at a price from both Arab traders and, sadly, African rulers. Writing from Arguin or Argin Island, off the coast of present-day Mauritania, in 1455, Alvise da Cadamosto, a Venetian explorer in the service of Prince Henry, gave a remarkably clear-eyed description of the mechanics of the trade:

> You should know that the said Lord Infante of Portugal [Prince Henry] has leased this island of Argin to Christians, so that no one can enter the bay to trade with the Arabs save those who hold the license. These have dwellings on the island and factories where they buy and sell with the said Arabs who come to the coast to trade for merchandise of various kinds, such as woollen cloths, cotton, silver, and *alchezeli*, that is, cloaks, carpets, and similar articles and above all, corn, for they are always short of food. They give in exchange slaves whom the Arabs bring from the land of the Blacks, and gold. The Lord Infante therefore caused a castle to be built on the island to protect his trade forever. For this reason, Portuguese caravels are coming and going all the year to this island . . . As a result every year the Portuguese carry away from Argin a thousand slaves.[5]

By the last two decades of the fifteenth century, upward of two thousand slaves were arriving annually to the markets of Portugal, and the sight of black Africans and their newly rich slavers on the streets of Lisbon was no longer a curiosity but a fact of Portuguese life.* Clearly, domestic service in the household of a noble or a well-off merchant as a washerwoman, say, or a liveryman was preferable to the toil of field work or the burden of moving merchandise on the Lisbon docks, but the fact remains that the fate of black slaves was almost always wretched, particularly in comparison with that of traditional white slaves (mostly enemies captured in battle), who enjoyed at least a modicum of rights. The defense against sexual exploitation granted to white female slaves, for example, was never respected with their black counterparts; masters were free to have their way with their African property whenever they fancied. The custom was nothing short of institutionalized rape, but the illegitimate offspring of these unholy master-slave unions were nonetheless born free and dutifully baptized into the Catholic Church. The long-term effect of this persistent miscegenation changed the countenance of the Portuguese forever. Other European nations such as Great Britain, France, and Holland would exploit slave labor in their colonies, but they never allowed the Africans to become a significant portion of the population in the mother countries. Not so the Portuguese. By the mid-eighteenth century, three hundred years after the first cargo of African slaves was brought to Portugal, the country had become a decidedly mixed bag racially. When foreign visitors characterized Lisbon as an "African city," it was to this racial amalgam that they were referring. The irony was inescapable; the Portuguese, who were among history's most enthusiastic slavers, managed over time to inadvertently create a mestizo society largely indifferent to race.

---

*The Portuguese surname Negreiro, that is, "one who trades in Negro slaves," is an eponymous vestige of the era.

CHAPTER FIVE

A GOLDEN AGE, OF SORTS

Arms and the heroes, who from Lisbon's shore,
Thro' seas where sail was never spread before,
Beyond where Ceylon lifts her spicy breast,
And waves her woods above the watery waste,
With prowess more than human forc'd their way
To the fair kingdoms of the rising day.

—Luís de Camões, *The Lusiads*

I t was adverse winds that first drove Portugal to Brazil. In 1500 King Manuel I, "the Fortunate," appointed Pedro Álvars Cabral to command a fleet to trace Vasco da Gama's pioneering voyage of 1497–98, in which the legendary mariner rounded the African Cape of Good Hope and discovered a direct sea route from Europe to the East. Cabral set sail from the Tagus on March 9 with a fleet of thirteen ships and fifteen hundred men and the express mission to develop trade with India by whatever means, preferably by alliance but if necessary by force. Off the coast of West Africa storms blew the fleet so far off course, however, that it reached the Brazilian coast (16 degrees southern latitude), where it dropped anchor, auspiciously, on Good Friday, April 24. On Easter Sunday mass was celebrated before the bewildered natives. Although the new territory was promptly declared a dominion of Portugal, Cabral appears to have shown little interest in the place. The crew made some cursory incursions into the tangled interior, gathered provisions and a few specimens of exotic plants and woods, and observed the heathen natives with a combination of curiosity and revulsion. On May 3 the fleet departed for India, its original destination, where there were riches in store. The only thing that Cabral and his men left behind in Brazil was a stone cross. The riches, of course, had been all around them, but it is obvious that Cabral knew nothing of what he had accidentally discovered and so hastily left behind.

The East beckoned, and Portugal was singularly well suited to exploit European society's fascination with all things oriental. For nearly a century after da Gama's epochal voyage, Portuguese carracks and caravels virtually monopolized the sea lane to Asia, and the country grew rich on the trade of Indian pepper and cotton, Indonesian perfume and spices, Chinese silk and porcelain, and African slaves, all of which passed through the royal trading house in Lisbon, the aptly named Casa da India. To defend the hegemony, Portugal took to empire building and, by the mid-sixteenth century, had conquered or colonized a string of scattered but strategic territories, including Angola, the Cape Verde Islands, Mozambique, Goa, Damão, and Macau. By sheer maritime prowess diminutive Portugal, like every great trading community from Carthage to Venice, had become an imperial power. Without the sea, the country would have been marginal at best. The Portuguese historian and poet Manuel de Faria e Sousa quoted a Chinese chronicler who had said of the Portuguese, "They are like fishes, remove them from the water and they straightaway die."

The magnitude of Portugal's newfound and precipitous wealth inspired a flowering of the arts, sciences, and literature, the likes of which the country had never known. Humanists such as the writer Damião de Goes, a friend to both Luther and Erasmus, was employed as the royal archivist and a diplomat, and his *Crónica* of the rule of King Manuel I was the first official history of a Portuguese reign to be written in a critical spirit. The playwright Gil Vicente, the greatest dramatist of the day and popular with the cultural elite and commoners alike, was also an accomplished musician, actor, and goldsmith. Advances in mathematics, astronomy, and

A pre-quake view of Lisbon shows a striking city rising from the banks of the Tagus. The multitude of vessels in the harbor is a testament to the robust trade that made Lisbon one of the busiest ports in Europe.

(Museu da Cidade, Câmara Municipal de Lisboa)

The Terreiro do Paço, hard by the royal palace, rendered by the Dutch painter Dirk Stoop nearly a century before the earthquake, fire, and tsunami laid waste to the palace and square.
(Museu da Cidade, Câmara Municipal de Lisboa)

An eighteenth-century French engraving entitled *Exécution des criminels condamnées par l'Inquisition* depicts the victims of an auto-da-fé and the multitudes that gathered to witness the grisly spectacle.

(*Museu da Cidade, Câmara Municipal de Lisboa*)

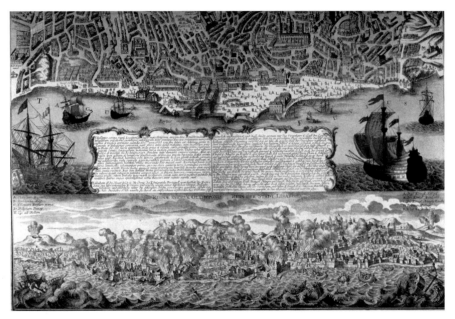

An eighteenth-century engraving from Germany originally utilized a brightly colored map to depict Lisbon before the earthquake and a grim black-and-white image of the city in the midst of the disaster.
(*Kozak Collection, EERC, University of California, Berkeley*)

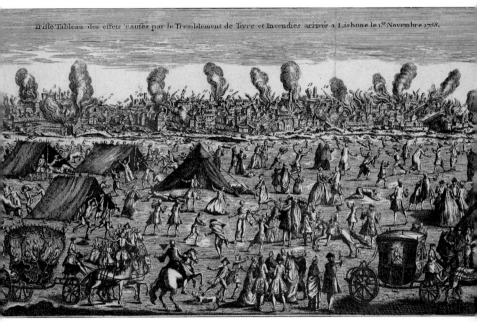

Triste Tableau des effets causés par le Tremblement de Terre et Incendies arrivés a Lisbone le 1.er Novembre 1755.

A French engraving from 1792 is scrupulous in recreating the chaos and havoc of the disaster, but it seems the artist cared little for topographical authenticity. The mighty Tagus is conspicuously absent.
(Museu da Cidade, Câmara Municipal de Lisboa)

A view from the south across the Tagus shows Lisbon in the throws of the triple disaster of earthquake, fire, and tsunami.
(*Kozak Collection, EERC, University of California, Berkeley*)

Many of the refugees, who attempted to flee the city by boat in the wake of the earthquake, as shown in this eighteenth-century Dutch engraving, met a watery grave as the subsequent tsunami battered the coast.
(Kozak Collection, EERC, University of California, Berkeley)

An oil painting by João Glama Stroberle from 1760 depicts a scene of pronounced piety as survivors pray for salvation beneath a legion of avenging angels. *(Kozak Collection, EERC, University of California, Berkeley)*

In the chaos that reigned in the immediate aftermath of the disaster, evildoers set upon the citizens of Lisbon, looting, robbing, and murdering at will.

(Kozak Collection, EERC, University of California, Berkeley)

The rescue and succor of victims during the earthquake and subsequent fire were not as evident as these engravings from 1793 would suggest.
(Kozak Collection, EERC, University of California, Berkeley)

A sea of refugee camps sprang up on the outskirts of Lisbon following the earthquake. Although lawlessness was initially rampant, a swift gallows justice was soon imposed to restore order, as seen in this German engraving from the period (*top*). The lower image shows the destruction in Meknes, Morocco.
(*Museu da Cidade, Câmara Municipal de Lisboa*)

Lisbon's cathedral in ruins, one of a series of engravings of the city's
shattered monuments produced by Jacques Philippe Le Bas, Paris,
1757.
(Kozak Collection, EERC, University of California, Berkeley)

Another of Le Bas's engravings shows the ruined Opera House, a magnificent
theater that had been inaugurated only six months before the quake.
(Kozak Collection, EERC, University of California, Berkeley)

In a British satirical illustration, King José of Portugal asks a Protestant clergyman how to avoid future manifestations of divine displeasure, to which the cleric responds by pointing to an image of the barbarity of the auto-da-fé and suggesting that His Majesty abolish the Inquisition.

(Kozak Collection, EERC, University of California, Berkeley)

A portrait of Sebastião José de Carvalho e Melo, better known to history as the Marquês de Pombal. His decisive handling of the disaster earned him the king's confidence and enabled him to rule Portugal for nearly twenty-seven years. (*Museu da Cidade, Câmara Municipal de Lisboa*)

Carvalho conferring with his collaborators on Lisbon's reconstruction, in an oil painting by M. A. Lupi.
(*Museu da Cidade, Câmara Municipal de Lisboa*)

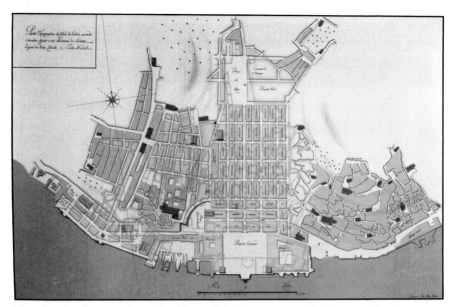

The plan for the complete rebuilding of the Baixa quarter by Eugénio dos Santos and Carlos Mardel was a model of enlightened eighteenth-century urban planning. (*Museu da Cidade, Câmara Municipal de Lisboa*)

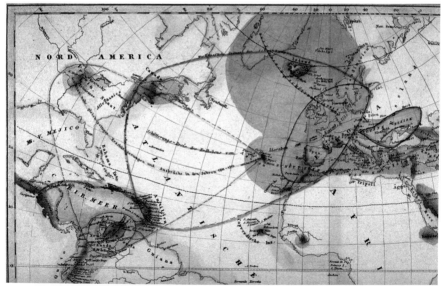

A map originally published in *Berghaus' physikalischer Atlas* (Gotha, 1849–1852) shows the expansive intercontinental area where the effects of the Lisbon earthquake were observed and recorded.
(*Kozak Collection, EERC, University of California, Berkeley*)

geography posed by Pedro Nunes (also known as Petrus Nonius) gave Portuguese explorers an edge in the new techniques of navigation. And in the arts a distinctive Renaissance-influenced school of painting, with Grão Vasco at its center, embellished churches, monasteries, and palaces that were being built on a scale and in quantities unprecedented for Portugal. Much of the new building was being designed in the unique High Gothic Manueline style (so called for King Manuel I), which was the architectural manifestation of the riches and ornamental exuberance to which the Portuguese had been exposed in the East. At the Jerónimos Monastery in Belém, commissioned by Manuel I to commemorate the discovery of the sea route to Asia and built between 1502 and 1525, both the interior and the exterior bear lavish surface decorations carved in stone with motifs of tropical fruits and flora, coral, buoys, ship rigging, globes, exotic fauna, and figures of mariners, all redolent of seafaring exploits and distant lands.* This combination of a new Renaissance spirit of inquiry and a kind of oriental luxuriance gave the social and cultural life of Lisbon a cosmopolitan air akin to that of Venice or Rome. While the quays moved the fruits of an empire, Lisbon's theaters, salons, libraries, and studios thrived.

The bonanza, alas, was as short lived as the decline was inevitable. Portugal's ills were legion and of the sort that incoming wealth, however startling, could only temporarily absolve. Most glaring was the sheer extent of the Portuguese Empire, which stretched from Brazil to the Malay Archipelago and required an enormous civil and military apparatus to administer and control. Emigration from the mother country to the colonies was draining

---

*Neither the Jerónimos Monastery nor the nearby Torre de Belém, another Manueline monument from the Age of Discovery, suffered serious damage from the earthquake.

Portugal of labor and initiative that were sorely needed at home. From approximately two million inhabitants in 1500, Portugal had lost nearly half of its population by 1586. Most of the emigrants traveled to Asia, of whom not one in ten is estimated to have returned; some succumbed to tropical disease, war, or shipwreck, while others simply stayed away by choice. Those who remained on the home front faced other menaces, including the Black Death and famine. During an especially virulent bout of the plague in 1569, for example, five hundred people died daily throughout the summer in Lisbon alone. To help redress the shortage of manpower, principally in agriculture, slaves were imported from West Africa to work the fields, but the measure only compounded the problem as local farmers felt degraded by association and abandoned the land for the towns and cities. The result was a proliferation of urban poor and increasingly frequent outbreaks of famine. At the height of its prosperity, the country was struggling to feed its own subjects.

Emigration may have been inevitable and the Black Death inescapable, but one of the costliest missteps of the monarchy during the late fifteenth and early sixteenth centuries had been entirely gratuitous, namely the persecution, forced conversion, and banishment of the Jews. For centuries Portuguese Jews had lived a relatively autonomous if frequently torturous existence. While tolerated by their Christian neighbors, Jews were also subject to a form of implacable and systematic discrimination that compelled them to live inside the Jewish quarters, or *Juderías* (read ghettos), to wear a badge distinguishing them from Gentiles, and to pay a special tax of thirty *dinheiros*, a spiteful allusion to the thirty pieces of silver paid to Judas Iscariot. Despite these humiliations, however, most Portuguese Jews were markedly more learned than Christian subjects. Lisbon boasted several Hebrew printing presses; many

Jews were well versed in Greek and Arabic philosophy and excelled in mathematics, astronomy, ~~finance~~ USURY, government, and medicine. Both King João II and his successor, Manuel I, entrusted their health to Jewish physicians; Vasco da Gama utilized nautical instruments supplied by the Jew Abraham ben Samuel Zacuto; and Jews were pivotal in promoting trade with Asia. They were, in short, the most dynamic and well-educated element of Portuguese society. Not surprisingly, it was the Church and the noble ranks that nurtured widespread anti-Semitism, the former for the fallacious blood debt for the death of Jesus Christ, the latter out of envy for the Jews' wealth and culture.

The Spanish monarchs Fernando and Isabel, *Los Reyes Católicos*, brought the matter to a head. Following the expulsion of the Moors and the Jews from Spain in 1492, close to 100,000 Jewish refugees were granted asylum in Portugal in exchange for a hefty poll tax, on condition that they leave the country within eight months, aboard ships to be provided by King João II. When these vessels failed to materialize, the Jewish refugees were enslaved, their families separated, and the children sent to work in the sugar plantations on the island of São Tomé in the Gulf of Guinea. In 1496 Manuel I, recently ascended to the Portuguese throne, sought the marriage of Isabella, daughter of Fernando and Isabel of Spain, in an effort to promote Iberian unity and consolidate a global empire. The Spanish monarchs favored the union in principle but imposed a sine qua non: Portugal had to rid its kingdom of the Jews. Needless to say, the economic and cultural repercussions of such an exodus would have been devastating to Portugal, so King Manuel I ordered every Jew to convert to Christianity or face exile to Africa. Scores of Jews committed suicide out of desperation, others submitted reluctantly to the new creed, and still others refused to renounce their faith and sailed into exile.

The forced converts became known as "New Christians" or, more vulgarly, as Marranos, but conversion hardly brought peace, and pogroms were common. During Holy Week in Lisbon in 1506, Dominican friars led an infuriated mob through the streets, seeking out and massacring most of the city's Jewish population, converts included; the bloodbath lasted for three days, and thousands were murdered. The introduction of the Holy Office of the Inquisition in 1536 only made matters worse. Dissidents, heretics, and "New Christians" suspected of Judaizing were the Inquisition's most common victims, and they were persecuted, prosecuted, and executed with hair-raising zeal. The fate of well-to-do Jews was especially precarious since the Inquisition paid its widespread network of informers out of the confiscated property of the condemned. A few poisonous words by an envious neighbor were enough to constitute a charge, and the accused were never permitted to face their accusers. By the middle of the sixteenth century Jews were emigrating in increasing numbers; they settled in the Levant, in North Africa, and in Holland, an oasis of religious tolerance in Christian Europe, where the Dutch welcomed them for their wealth, enterprise, and culture. Soon enough, Portugal's self-inflicted loss became Holland's gain, as Dutch traders, greatly assisted by Jewish capital, contacts, and commercial acumen, became among the Portuguese's most dogged rivals in global trade.*

---

*The descendents of many of these Jews of the sixteenth- and seventeenth-century exodus, among them the philosopher Baruch Spinoza, found fertile ground in Holland. Few, however, made good quite so splendidly as Isaac de Pinto (1717–87), who helped to found the United East India Company and became one of the wealthiest men in Amsterdam. The Italianate Pintohuis on Sint Antoniesbreestraat, now a public library, was the family's palatial residence.

At least since the Middle Ages the Catholic Church had been employing an inquisitional body of one sort or another as a means to suppress heresy and preserve the unity of Christendom. These medieval tribunals, however, tended to be both localized and temporary, arising wherever and whenever a particularly egregious doctrinal deviation threatened to grow into a full-scale religious rebellion. The most notorious of these early inquisitional campaigns was launched against the Albigensian heresy in southern France in the twelfth and thirteenth centuries; thousands of Cathari, or suspected Cathari, who professed vehemently anti-clerical doctrines in defiance of *any* ecclesiastical authority, were mercilessly slaughtered. The Holy Office of the Inquisition, which was established in Spain in the late fifteenth century and imported to Portugal in 1536, however, was different from any other previous inquisitional tribunal in that it was answerable to the Crown alone rather than to the pope, and its activities had as much to do with wielding the power of the state in the aftermath of the Reconquest as with safeguarding the doctrinal purity of the faith. The Inquisition's systematic use of torture, show trials, and ghastly public autos-da-fé constituted a highly effective regimen of institutionalized terror and contributed to the emergence of the so-called Black Legend, which portrayed all of Iberia as cast beneath a mantle of fanaticism, bigotry, violence, and death.

In truth, no one propagated the Black Legend quite so resolutely as Protestant propagandists, but institutions such as the Inquisition gave them an exceedingly easy time of it. The abuses of the Holy Office, or the Santo Oficio as it was known, were described in excruciating detail in a flood of books and pamphlets published in northern Europe in the sixteenth century, but few were quite so successful in fomenting anti-Catholic prejudice or so enduring in their influence as John Foxe's *Book of Martyrs*

(1554 in Latin, 1563 in English) and *Sanctae Inquisitionis Hispanicae Artes* (*A Discovery and Plaine Declaration of Sundry Subtill Practices of the Holy Inquisition of Spain*), published in 1567 by the pseudonymous author Reginaldus Gonsalvus Montanus.* In a good many staunchly Protestant households in northern Europe, the British Isles, and the American colonies, the *Book of Martyrs* and Montanus were among the few works, apart from the Bible, that ordinary families cared to have under their roofs. Although Foxe's book comprised an exhaustive chronicle of Christian persecution from the reign of Nero to that of England's queen "Bloody Mary," some of the work's most hair-raising scenes were devoted to the practices and proceedings of the Spanish and Portuguese Inquisitions, and they would instill abhorrence for all things Catholic in Protestant consciences for centuries. Foxe spared few details, for example, in the elaborate mechanisms of torture to which an anonymous survivor had been submitted in the Inquisition's prison in Lisbon:

> The inquisitors allow the torture to be used only three times, but during those times it is so severely inflicted, that the prisoner either dies under it, or continues always after a cripple . . .
>
> At the first time of torturing, six executioners entered, stripped him naked to his drawers, and laid him upon his back on a kind of stand, elevated a few feet from the floor. The operation commenced by putting an iron collar round his neck, and a ring to each foot, which fastened him to the stand. His limbs being thus

---

*In all likelihood Montanus was the pseudonym of Antonio del Coro, a theologian and ex-monk from Seville's San Isidro Monastery who had converted to Calvinism and lived in exile in Antwerp.

stretched out, they wound two ropes around each thigh; which ropes being passed under the scaffold, through holes made for that purpose, were all drawn tight at the same instant of time, by four men, on a given signal.

It is easy to conceive that the pains which immediately succeeded were intolerable; the ropes, which were of a small size, cut through the prisoner's flesh to the bone, making the blood gush out at eight different places thus bound at a time. As the prisoner persisted in not making any confession of what the inquisitors required, the ropes were drawn in this manner four times successively.[1]

This legally sanctioned barbarity—heresy being a civil crime and torture a common feature of eighteenth-century jurisprudence—continued on two subsequent visits to the torture chamber with ever more macabre means of torment, until the victim, resolute in proclaiming his innocence, was released "crippled and diseased for life." But he was among the lucky ones. For those who were condemned to an auto-da-fé in the Rossio square, the nightmare was prolonged with a ritual of public humiliation, spiritual cleansing, and death. The victims, already decimated by the rack and the dungeon, were paraded before the throng wearing the *san benito*, a penitential tunic or scapular of plain yellow cloth, and the high conical cap known as the *coroza*. In their hands they clutched candles. Each *san benito* was painted with a portrait of its wearer and additional images that defined his fate: if the tunic was adorned with a cross, then the individual was sentenced only to do additional penance; if the *san benito* was painted with images of flames that extended downward, it signaled that the penitent had undergone a hasty conversion and thus had the privilege of being strangled prior to being burned; if the victim was an unrepentant heretic, Judaizer, Protestant, mystic, or witch, the *san benito* bore a flourish of flames, dragons, and devils, indicating that this *impenitente* was to be burned alive.* Before the victim was strangled and/or confined to the flames, however, solemn prayers were offered; a thunderous sermon was preached to a morbidly animated crowd, which often numbered in the thousands; and the final sentence was read by a priestly inquisitor:

> We, the inquisitors of heretical pravity, having, with the concurrence of the most illustrious ———, lord archbishop of Lisbon . . . calling on the name of the Lord Jesus Christ, and his glorious mother, the Virgin Mary, and sitting on our tribunal, and judging with the holy gospels lying before us, so that our judgement may be in the sight of God, and our eyes may behold what is just in all matters . . . We do therefore, by this our sentence put in writing, define, pronounce, declare, and sentence thee (the prisoner), of the city of Lisbon, to be convicted, confessing, affirmative, and professed heretic; and to be delivered and left by us as such to the secular arm; and we, by this our sentence, do cast thee out of the ecclesiastical court as a convicted, confessing, affirmative, and professed heretic; and we do leave and deliver thee to the secular arm, and to the power of the secular court, but at the same

---

*The *san benitos*, painted with the portrait of each penitent, were often hung in display in the Church of São Domingos as a further disgrace to the family of the victim and as a chilling reminder to the populace of the price of heresy.

time do most earnestly beseech that court so to moderate its sentence as not to touch thy blood, nor to put
thy life in any sort of danger.[2]

By turning the condemned over to the secular court, the Church
undoubtedly attempted to soothe a bloodstained conscience, but
it did little to deflect its ultimate responsibility. In matters pertaining to the faith, the temporal powers were largely beholden to the
ecclesiastical order and were required to act against heresy. In earnestly beseeching the court not to touch the victim's blood, the
inquisitors were making a hollow entreaty, and the result was invariably the same—the fires were kindled, and a priest was allowed
to utter a final calumny, telling the writhing wretches at the stake
that the devil was waiting to receive their souls and carry them to
the flames of hell. Amen.

That the Inquisitions of Spain and Portugal were abominations
is beyond dispute; any misguided attempt to coerce human conscience by an exterminating sword, however lofty the motive—
in this case, nothing less ambitious than the unity of all of
Christendom—is in itself antithetical. The Inquisition was emi-
nently deserving of every denunciation that came its way, and yet
the clamor of Protestants purporting to be shocked by the religious
intolerance of Iberia, and to be shaken by the tales of implacable
torture and ritualized executions, was at once self-serving and hyp-
ocritical. As weapons in the religious propaganda war of the sixteenth century, works such as Foxe's *Book of Martyrs* were a potent
force, but these diatribes remained mostly silent or scandalously
benevolent on the terrors that were unfolding in the Protestant
world in the name of the reformed faith. The persecution of heretics was not a Catholic invention; indeed it could be traced to
Mosaic Law: "Whoever curses his God shall bear his sin. He who

blasphemes the name of the Lord shall be put to death; all the congregation shall stone him; the sojourner as well as the native, when he blasphemes the Name, shall be put to death" (Leviticus 24:15–16). What Roman Catholicism came to countenance in the name of orthodoxy was murderous, but the very concept of heresy for a Protestant was especially troublesome since Protestantism emerged, above all, in defense of the right and freedom of interpretation. Nonetheless, in Protestant societies of the sixteenth century heretics too could be imprisoned, exiled, stripped of their property, tortured, hanged, decapitated, or burned at the stake. Luther explicitly condoned capital punishment for unrepentant heretics; so too did Melanchthon, not to speak of Calvin. While Protestant propaganda was busy skewering "Romanish" fanaticism, religious persecution in John Calvin's Geneva had transformed the once somnolent provincial capital into a theocratic city-state:

> Prohibited were theatres, amusements, popular festivals, any kind of dancing or playing. Even so innocent a sport as skating stirred Calvin's bile. The only tolerated attire was sober and almost monkish. The tailors, therefore, were forbidden, unless they had special permission from the town authorities, to cut in accordance with new fashions. Girls were forbidden to wear silk before they reached the age of fifteen years; above that age, they were not allowed to wear velvet . . . Lace was forbidden; gloves were forbidden; frills and slashed shoes were forbidden. Forbidden was the use of litters and of wheeled carriages. Forbidden were family feasts to which more than twenty persons

had been invited . . . No other wine than the red wine of the region might be drunk, while game, whether four footed or winged, and pastry, were prohibited. Married folk were not allowed to give one another presents at the wedding, or for six months afterward . . . No book might be printed without a special permit . . . Forbidden as a crime of crimes was any criticism of Calvin's dictatorship; and the town crier, preceded by drummers, solemnly warned the burghers that "there must be no discussion of public affairs except in the presence of the Town Council."[3]

And naturally in this morose Swiss "City of God" heresy was forbidden. During the first five years of Calvin's rule, from 1541 to 1546, thirteen people were hanged, ten decapitated, thirty-five burned at the stake, and seventy-six driven into exile, all for opposing Calvinist doctrines. In 1553 Michael Servetus, a Spanish-born theologian and Protestant convert with less than orthodox views, arrived in Geneva seeking an audience with Calvin, who promptly had him arrested. He was charged with heresy for having denied the Trinity and burned at the stake.

The Calvinist terror was hardly typical, it's true, but elsewhere in Protestant Europe religious tolerance was far from the norm. The death penalty for heresy was stricken from the statute books in England only in 1677. As late as 1697 an eighteen-year-old student named Thomas Aikenhead was hanged in Edinburgh for having purportedly derided Christ as an impostor and rejected the Trinity, the Incarnation, and the Redemption. And in Puritan Salem, Massachusetts, nineteen victims were hanged and another pressed to death in the witchcraft delusion of 1692. It can be argued that these Protestant crimes were occasional and localized, while the Inquisitions of Portugal and Spain, by contrast, were entrenched, unchecked institutions that operated with uncommon zeal and efficiency for centuries. This is undoubtedly true. The sheer degree of religious persecution in Iberia was markedly worse than that of Protestant societies. From the Inquisition's inception in Portugal in 1536 to the last auto-da-fé in Lisbon in 1765, the Holy Office tried some forty thousand cases and condemned nearly two thousand *impenitente* to death; thousands more were victims of torture, exile, and economic ruin. Understandably, this is the stuff of which stigmas are made.

Alas, it wasn't just heretics and recalcitrant Jews who concerned the Holy Office, although they were by far its most prevalent victims. The pursuit of religious orthodoxy drove the Inquisition to institute a system of unbridled censorship, which stifled any new ideas perceived to threaten Church authority. All printed matter, prior to publication; had to be reviewed by the Inquisition's censors, whose criteria were decidedly less than enlightened. While poetry and romances customarily passed censor, historical works were often butchered to conform to ecclesiastical exegeses, and all new philosophical or scientific tracts were banned outright. The relentless scrutiny smothered intellectual inquiry and had a devastating effect on higher education. At the University of Coimbra, one of Europe's oldest (established in 1308) and most prestigious universities, where the country's elite was groomed for power, censorship threatened to reduce the curriculum to the traditional medieval study of theology, canon law, civil law, and medicine. Lectures on mathematics, philosophy, logic, and the natural sciences were duly silenced. In 1547 the Scottish humanist and poet George Buchanan was lecturing at Coimbra when he was denounced and hauled before the tribunal

of the Inquisition, accused of Lutheran and Judaistic practices.*
The charges, Buchanan admitted, were not entirely unfounded,
and he proceeded to make an impassioned defense of religious
tolerance and the spiritual legacy of the Jews. The inquisitors,
however, were deaf to reform, let alone freedom of conscience,
and rabidly anti-Semitic, and Buchanan was sentenced to recant
his theological errors and be imprisoned in Lisbon's Monastery of
São Bento. For seven months he was submitted to edifying sermons from the Benedictine monks, whom he regarded as "not
unkind but ignorant," before he was finally released.

The whole affair was indicative of what awaited open minds
and visiting scholars in Portugal, and the lengths to which the
Inquisition was willing to go in order to preserve Catholic orthodoxy. By midcentury the entire educational system was put in
the hands of the Society of Jesus, or Jesuits, the recently formed
militant order that had assumed the educational mission of the
Counter-Reformation. The University of Coimbra was purged
of free thinkers, and in 1558 the Jesuits established their own
university at Évora, where the syllabus included Aristotle, Augustine, Boethius, and especially Aquinas, for his emphasis on obedience; Erasmus, Copernicus, and Wycliffe were noticeably
absent. And so as to prevent the vernacular literature that was
sweeping Europe from corrupting the young minds of Portugal,
the Jesuits insisted on teaching exclusively in Latin. The effect of
this conservative reaction on the education of the Portuguese was
predictable enough: while much of northern Europe was giddy
with a newfound humanist and religious spirit, Portugal slipped
silently back to the Middle Ages.

---

*Nor did it help Buchanan's cause that he was the author of the well-known
poem *Somnium*, a satirical attack on the Franciscans and monastic life in
general.

Ecclesiastical control of education and the tribunals would not have been possible without the overt support of the monarchy. Under the reign of Manuel I (1495–1521), the Catholic Church was never allowed to intrude on the royal prerogative, but Manuel's son and successor, João III, was made of more fervid stuff. Although João III assumed the throne at the zenith of Portugal's empire, he rarely summoned the Cortes (Parliament) for consultation, and his rule was increasingly determined by the influence of his ecclesiastical advisers. It was he who petitioned Rome to introduce the Holy Office of the Inquisition to Portugal, and it was he who allowed the institution to effectively grow into a state within a state. When João III died in 1557 without a son to succeed him, the throne passed to his grandson, Sebastião, age three. While the child king was being groomed for power by Jesuit tutors, the country was ruled by a joint regency comprised of Queen Catarina, a fanatical daughter of Isabel the Catholic, and Prince Henrique, a cardinal and Portugal's inquisitor general. The separation of Church and Crown was all but nonexistent.

Sebastião was headstrong but weak-minded, a fatal condition for a monarch, and his brief reign was marked by a near total subservience to his Jesuit entourage. Although he was, along with his great-uncle Cardinal Henrique, the only legitimate male heir to the House of Aviz, which had ruled Portugal since the late fourteenth century, Sebastião bore an ascetic streak and refused emphatically to marry. His passions lay rather in imperial aggrandizement and Crusade; his most cherished hero was Don Juan of Austria, who defeated the Turks at the great naval battle of Lepanto in 1571. At a time when the Portuguese Empire was sapping the mother country of both manpower and funds, Sebastião embarked on a Crusade against the infidels of Morocco in an attempt to revive his country's fortunes. The bulk of the Portuguese army was defending the country's distant conquests in Asia, but Sebastião extorted the "New Christians" to pay for a ragtag force comprised of boy soldiers, weary veterans, and assorted mercenaries. In the summer of 1578 Sebastião set sail from Lisbon with eighteen thousand men and an inordinate desire to smite the Moors. Landing at Arzila, Sebastião proclaimed Morocco a Portuguese suzerainty and proceeded overland to meet the Muslim armies. After an infernal desert march under an August sun, Sebastião and his force made camp near Alcácer-Quivir and on the morning of August 4 were surrounded and outnumbered by the army of Sultan Abd Al-Malik. It was a rout. Sebastião was killed and his army virtually annihilated in one of the most foolhardy episodes in Portuguese history. What's more, chaste Sebastião left no heir, the House of Aviz was wasted, and the country braced for a battle of succession.*

It was just the twist of fate that Spain had been eagerly awaiting. The unification of the Iberian Peninsula had been proceeding slowly but inexorably since the Christian Reconquest began in the eighth century. The ancient kingdom of Asturias had been united with that of León, León with Castile, Castile with Aragon and Catalonia and Andalusia. The only holdout was Portugal. The claimants to the Portuguese throne included Catarina, Duquesa de Bragança; António, prior of Crato; Ranuccio, Duke of Parma; Philibert, Duke of Savoy; and Felipe II, King of Spain. In fact, there was little contest where power and influence were concerned; Felipe II, the Habsburg claimant, had the overwhelming

---

*No sooner had news of the defeat reached Portugal than rumor spread asserting that Sebastião had survived the battle and would one day return and restore the former glory of the country. In time the rumor grew into a kind of messianic cult known as Sebastianism, which boasted thousands of votaries. Over the centuries scores of impostors arose claiming to be the *rei encuberto*, or "hidden king."

support of the Catholic Church, especially the Jesuits, and more important still, he had the military might of Spain to back him up. In 1581 he sent an army across the Portuguese frontier under the Duke of Alba and defeated a band of loyalists at Alcântara. Soon afterward Felipe II, who adopted the Portuguese title of Filipe I, was crowned king; the unification of Iberia was complete; and Spain was the lord of a world empire that stretched from the West Indies to the East Indies.

Spain did not enter Portugal entirely as an interloper. Indeed, from a dynastic point of view, Felipe's claim to the throne was legitimate enough. Many Portuguese advocated the union, and many others simply saw it as logical or at least inevitable. Wisely, Felipe II trod delicately with regard to Portuguese autonomy and was careful not to wound the nation's pride. By the Council of Tomar, which formalized the union in 1581, Spain agreed to regard Portugal not as conquered territory but as a separate kingdom, and its colonies in Asia, Africa, and Brazil were to remain Portuguese. The Cortes would be convened regularly (something that had scarcely occurred since the death of Manuel I in 1521), and a Portuguese privy council would be consulted on issues pertaining to Portugal. The advantages of the union were both practical and far-reaching. To begin with, the Portuguese-Spanish frontier, whose defense had for centuries absorbed a disproportionate amount of manpower and resources, was suddenly open (much to the consternation of smugglers, horse thieves, arms dealers, and the like). Portuguese traders saw their potential markets grow tenfold; and the Portuguese court was at once exposed to the more sophisticated and powerful court of Spain. On a popular level, sentiments of cultural patriotism rooted in a distinct language and history seemed moot. No uprisings ensued; no rebellions formed; no conspiracies hatched, for the moment.

The realization of the liabilities of unification was not long in coming. Portuguese diplomacy had always actively sought out allies to avoid military confrontations with the larger European states. The country had no territorial claims in Europe and had never attempted aggrandizement on the Continent. Remarkably, Portugal's frontiers had not changed since the fall of the Muslims' "Kingdom of the West" in the Algarve in the mid-thirteenth century. By association with Spain, however, Portugal had suddenly garnered a host of powerful enemies, including England, France, and Holland, and both the Portuguese mainland and its diffuse colonies were now exposed to hostile incursions. The English sacked Faro in the Algarve in 1596 and the Azores a year later. The English, French, and Dutch were all making inroads in Brazil and took to regularly engaging or harassing the Portuguese fleet. In the East, the Dutch attacked the Portuguese in Ceylon in 1601 and a year later defeated a powerful Portuguese fleet off Banda in the Moluccas. In 1608 Holland forced Portugal to sign a humbling twelve-year armistice that provided the former with carte blanche to expand her Asian trade at the latter's expense. By the early seventeenth century Portugal was no longer supreme at sea, nor did it enjoy a monopoly of the Asian sea route or the markets of the East. Moreover, as little more than an appendage of Spain, Portugal found itself unable to negotiate independent treaties or separate peaces. Portugal had become hostage to Spanish fortunes, and the much-trumpeted union began to look less like a historic opportunity than a not-too-subtle national capitulation.

It was Iberian events that provided the catalyst for a Portuguese rebellion. By 1640 Portugal had lived under three Spanish monarchs, and the formalities of the Tomar agreement were just so much empty rhetoric. The Cortes had met only twice in almost

sixty years, Portugal had succumbed to a humiliating Castilianiza-
tion, and the country was relentlessly taxed and drained of able-
bodied men to fight Spanish battles against the French in the
Thirty Years' War. There wasn't a class in Portuguese society that
had not been somehow wronged by Spanish policies. Nobles were
jealous of the influx and influence of Spanish courtiers; landowners resented the burden of Spanish taxes and the loss of their best
field hands to military conscription. Merchants and traders saw
once-flourishing colonial territories collapse and much of their
precious cargoes intercepted by foreign rivals. Even the Jesuits,
the most vociferous champions of Iberian unification, began to
contemplate throwing off the Spanish yoke. The spark of mutiny
came from Catalonia, Spain's historically contentious province
in the northeast. In the summer of 1640 the Catalans rebelled
against Felipe IV and his minister the Duque de Olivares for much
the same motives that had inspired the ire of the Portuguese:
forced military conscription, abusive levels of taxation, and a
thorough disregard for centuries-old local rights and customs. Felipe IV turned once again to Portugal and ordered an army raised
to march across the breadth of the peninsula and snuff the Cata-
lan insurrection in the east.

The Portuguese refused. It was not a grassroots revolt but
rather an act of defiance by the great landowners of the central
plains of Portugal, who could ill afford further military levies and
balked at putting down a fellow Iberian people with whom they
had no quarrel.* The Portuguese seized the moment, knowing
very well that Spanish troops would be unable to fight rebellions

---

*A genuinely grassroots, peasant revolt against Spanish policies sprang up in
Évora in 1637, but the initiative lacked organization and the support of the
middle class and nobles and was quickly and brutally crushed.

on two fronts. A conspiratorial band of disaffected nobles inspired by João Pinto Ribeiro, a professor at the University of Coimbra, approached João, the Duque de Bragança and a descendant of Manuel I, to lead the revolt and restore Portuguese independence. The duque, however, was indolent by nature and understandably wary of the rebellion. The Bragança family was the richest in Portugal and the country's greatest private landowner; if the plot failed, they stood to lose everything. João, not surprisingly, vacillated, but he was eventually brought around by, of all people, his Spanish wife, Doña Luisa de Guzmán. On December 1 the rebels forced their way into the Paço da Ribeira and ousted the resident authority of the Spanish Crown, Margaret of Savoy, Duchess of Mantua, and her bloated train of Spanish and Italian courtiers. The Spanish garrisons, vastly undermanned, offered little resistance and the soldiers were expelled. On December 13 the Duque de Bragança was crowned João IV (history would dub him "the Restorer") and was promptly recognized by England, France, and Holland, the same powers that had so relentlessly attacked Portugal under Spanish rule. Spain, alas, was powerless to prevent the Portuguese restoration; the Castilian armies were too busy suppressing the Catalans on the far side of the peninsula. The sixty-year Babylonian Captivity ended with barely a drop of blood spilled, and Portugal was independent once again. Catalonia, by contrast, felt the full weight of Castilian retribution and was eventually starved into submission.

Portuguese independence had been achieved swiftly, almost effortlessly, but it would prove short-lived unless Portugal could find a protector among the major powers. France had actively supported Portugal's break from Spain, not out of any altruistic notion of statecraft but for its debilitating effect on her Spanish archrival. Once the Portuguese restoration was complete, however, France was largely indifferent to the country's fate. The height of French cynicism came in 1647 when Cardinal Mazarin, the foreign minister of Louis XIV, actually offered the Portuguese throne to his friend the Duke of Longueville; nothing ever came of the plot, but it proved the extent of Portugal's vulnerability. The Dutch too were quick to acknowledge Portuguese independence, but commercial rivalry in Asia, Africa, and Brazil was the source of constant tension and frequent armed hostilities, and a solid alliance seemed implausible.* As for the English, Charles I was dealing with a rebellion of his own by the Scots and had come to a deadlock with Parliament. Clearly, he had little time or resources to placate the Portuguese. Portugal would have to tough it out alone, and by and large the country didn't do a bad job of it. Until his death in 1656 João IV managed to repel various attempts by Spain to reconquer the country. Portugal also finally succeeded in driving the Dutch out of Brazil in 1654 and turned the colony into a principality in which the heir apparent to the Portuguese throne was invested with the title Prince of Brazil. In spite of the cost of ousting the Dutch and the exactions by Portugal, Brazil was growing steadily more prosperous. Brazilian sugar, tobacco, wood, coffee, and hides were all trading briskly in the markets of Europe, and the revenues helped to offset the Portuguese losses in Asia.

The search for a stalwart ally with the maritime muscle to help defend Portugal's foreign domains was at last settled, as alliances so often were in seventeenth-century Europe, by a propitious marriage. In 1661 Catarina, the daughter of João IV, was offered in marriage to Charles II of England. (She had first been proffered to Louis XIV, *Le Roi Soleil*, but the marriage negotiations failed.)

---

*In 1641 the Dutch captured Luanda in West Africa, Portugal's most extensive slaving grounds, and held it for seven years.

The nuptial arrangements were set down in an Anglo-Portuguese treaty that prepared the way for ever closer relations between the two countries. Catarina's dowry was no pittance: in addition to two million pieces of gold, Portugal threw in Tangiers and Bombay to boot.* It was, by Portugal's reckoning, a small price to pay for survival. Henceforth England pledged to protect Portugal on land and sea, which is to say, from Spain and Holland, and the Portuguese could attempt to restore their country's sinking fortunes. By the mid-seventeenth century Portugal's Asian and African empires had entered their twilight, and the country set its gaze and its hopes across the Atlantic on the vast potential of Brazil.

In the late 1690s a band of Portuguese explorers, fortune hunters, and slavers happened upon expansive goldfields in the Brazilian district of Minas Gerais. The discovery ignited a gold rush of white plantation owners and their native and African slaves, as well as any luckless Portuguese with an insatiable desire to get rich quick in the lawless mining camps of the Brazilian interior. Thousands joined the tide, especially those from Portugal's impoverished northern provinces who were living in near feudal conditions and had, quite literally, nothing to lose. To no one's surprise, they took to mining with relish. In 1700 the mines produced 50,000 ounces of gold, something of a mother lode; five years later the bounty had soared to 600,000 ounces. Soon more goldfields were unearthed in Mato Grosso, followed by a new discovery, that of diamonds and a constellation of other precious stones. Brazil, the jewel in the Portuguese Crown, began to resemble the true El Dorado. The golden age of Portugal had begun, and it was no mere metaphor.

---

*The ability of a dowry to mark the course of history is only too apparent when one considers that the ceding of Bombay gave England its first foothold on the Indian subcontinent.

João V ascended the throne in 1707, just in time to reap the rewards of the Brazilian bonanza. By law, the royal coffers received one-fifth of all gold production; diamonds in excess of twenty carats were deemed *regalia,* or gifts for the monarch. The Portuguese royal family promptly became one of the wealthiest in Europe, but seldom had the kingdom prospered less. The enormous quantities of bullion imported by the treasury were used principally to wage war alternately on the Spaniards, the French, and the Turks, to slavishly mimic the pomp of the French court at Versailles, and to lavish the pope and the Church with untold riches. When the king did address a problem in the realm, his response was invariably the same; he handed out gold coins minted with his effigy. Such royal munificence could alleviate a host of minor if vexing troubles, but it did nothing to solve Portugal's historic social and economic shortcomings. While the Portuguese treasure ships continued to arrive in Lisbon laden with Brazilian riches, the country, or rather the Crown, was blind to the backwardness that plagued the kingdom. It didn't seem to matter. If agriculture had grown impoverished due to the exodus of emigrants to the Brazilian gold rush (just as it had in the sixteenth century with the rush to Asia), corn and wheat could always be imported. Industries such as textiles were ignored in favor of imported British fabrics. The wealthiest monarchy in Europe, said Portugal's critics, could not feed or clothe its own subjects. They had a point, but as long as the revenues from gold, diamonds, sugar, tobacco, and slaves kept flowing, no one seemed to worry; nor were they asked. The riches of Brazil allowed the Portuguese Crown to govern without summoning the Cortes to vote supply for the treasury. The Cortes convened in 1697, just as gold was discovered in Brazil, and it would not be summoned again until 1822.

João V was first among the faithful and bore the title of *Fidelis-simus*, or "Most Faithful," an honor that Pope Benedict XIV be-stowed upon the monarch for the aid of Portuguese ships in the Crusade against the Turks. The new title put the king of Portugal on par with his Most Christian Majesty of France and his Most Catholic Majesty of Spain. João's piety was renowned throughout Europe and not above mockery. "This monarch's gaieties were re-ligious processions," wrote Voltaire. "When he took to building, he built monasteries, and when he wanted a mistress, he chose a nun."[4] The characterization was apt. The princes Gaspar and José, later to become the archbishop of Braga and the grand in-quisitor, respectively, were both illegitimate, born to nuns in the convent of Odivelas, a favorite stomping ground, it would seem, of the less-than-prudish king.

But it was as the builder of monasteries, convents, churches, chapels, and episcopal palaces that João V would forge his legacy and, no doubt, soothe his conscience. Armed with a portentous faith and a treasury swollen with Brazilian gold, he went on a building frenzy for the glory of God and his own majesty. When the king decided that Lisbon's Church of São Roque needed a chapel dedicated to John the Baptist, he commissioned the Ital-ian architects Luigi Vanvitelli and Nicola Salvi to build the struc-ture in their studio in Rome (that it might be blessed by the pope) before transporting it to the Portuguese capital. No expense, indi-cated the king, was to be spared. The architects took the monarch at his word and employed eighteen types of marble, four varieties of alabaster, ormolu, porphyry, agate, lapis lazuli, amethyst, gilded sculpture and wood, silver filigree, mosaics, and paintings. The whole lot was shipped to Lisbon and assembled by Italian crafts-men. The diminutive chapel, measuring seventeen feet by twelve feet, cost an astonishing quarter of a million pounds, and Europe was abuzz with rumor and envy of the excesses of the spendthrift Portuguese king.

Nothing, however, captures João's dual penchant for extravagance and piety quite so well as his scheme for a colossal palace-convent at Mafra, on the barren plain northwest of Lisbon. It was an unlikely site for a royal palace, but in fact the location was the result of a vow made in the confessional. If provided with a legitimate heir, João had proclaimed to his confessor, he swore to transform the country's humblest monastery into a monument of unparalleled splendor. When the queen, Archduchess Maria Ana of Austria, gave birth to Prince José Manuel in 1714, the king's vow came due, and Mafra, an obscure Franciscan monastery with a handful of friars, was tapped for the royal patronage. Designed by the German silversmith-turned-architect Johann Friedrich Ludwig (Ludovice, in the Latinized form), the Mafra complex represented the height of the Portuguese baroque, although in plan it was modeled after Felipe II's severe Escorial Palace in Spain. Built between 1715 and 1735, the edifice came to employ fifty thousand workmen and its cost exceeded four million pounds, a scandalous expenditure by the measure of any monarch of the day. It had nearly a thousand rooms, from gilt-filled royal chambers to Spartan monks' cells. Tellingly, the royal apartments flanked the domed church at the center of the principal facade, thus creating a seamless proximity of God and Crown. Mafra was the architectural embodiment of a gilded age of faith, but for all its indisputable grandeur, it was a hollow confection, financed by the infernal, slave-driven mines of Brazil.

The squandering of riches on the Church, the war, and the royal family and its retinue left little revenue to improve the condition of the average Portuguese. The reign of João V is often cited as a period of artistic and literary renaissance, which indeed it was, but it was a blossoming by and for the cultural elite. The royal library, which the king so painstakingly endowed, for example, and the magnificent library at the University of Coimbra, which he commissioned, were admirable initiatives, but he undertook no corresponding development of public education or popular literacy. Public primary and secondary schools were unknown, and those administered by religious orders such as the Jesuits educated the children of the patrician class. The vast majority of the country's subjects, especially in rural areas, were woefully ignorant, which was, by and large, how the Church, the Crown, and the nobility preferred them.

Living conditions for the masses were no less bleak. During the building boom that swept Lisbon in the first half of the eighteenth century, nobles and merchant princes built scores of palaces and elegant townhouses; the Palácio Barbacena, the Italianate Palácio Ludovice, and the Quinta das Águias, among others, gave the capital an air of opulence that it had never known. The king, undeterred by the cost and resources expended on Mafra, also commissioned the royal retreat at Belém; the sprawling, baroque Palácio das Necessidades in western Lisbon; and the Palácio Galvão Mexia in the Campo Grande, on the northern outskirts of the capital. (The last was built for his mistress, Mother Paula of the Odivelas convent.) But hard by many of these sumptuous residences, with their fine French-inspired furniture, radiant chandeliers, picture galleries, libraries, and sequestered gardens of parterres, fountains, and dizzying *azulejos*, lived the masses of poor in warrens and hovels of medieval decrepitude. Open sewers fouled the unpaved streets; disease and vermin were ubiquitous. One of the few public works undertaken during João V's reign was the Aqueduto das Águas Livres, which finally brought fresh water to the capital, but the project was only partially funded by the king—the lion's share of the cost was borne by the residents of Lisbon.

As for industry, it was virtually nonexistent. Portuguese trade had historically sought commercial profit in the acquisition of gold and silver rather than in an exchange of commodities. Portuguese merchants unloaded raw materials in the ports of Holland, England, Germany, and France, where they were used to establish productive industries that contributed to a broader-based wealth. Ironically, many of the merchants in Holland who established sugar refineries, tobacco-processing plants, goldsmith firms, and diamond-cutting businesses, all of which depended significantly on Portugal for raw materials, were prominent Portuguese Jewish exiles like the Pereira, Pinto, Barrios, and Pina families. In Portugal there was little such trickling-down effect, nor such diversification. Some enterprising Portuguese burghers, for example, had tried to develop a national textile industry in the seventeenth century, but opposition from archconservative landowners and the Church squashed the enterprise. The result was that many burghers fled en masse to Brazil and subsequently thrived, leaving Portugal further deprived of commercial acumen and obliged to import finished fabrics from abroad. By the Treaty of Methuen, which Portugal signed with England in 1703, Portugal admitted English textiles duty free and England imported Portuguese wine at a greatly reduced tariff. The treaty resulted in the rapid domination of Portuguese trade by the British (textiles were Portugal's single largest import commodity), but little benefit accrued to Portugal, except a stable market for a traditional monoculture. Plainly, it was gold alone that kept the monarchy and the country afloat and allowed the reckoning to be postponed. During the forty-three years of João V's rule (1707–50), an estimated five hundred tons of Brazilian gold landed on the Lisbon quays, but the bounty was rarely shared. The king may well have had "more gold stored up, coined and uncoined, than all the other princes of Europe together," as John Wesley claimed, but the only gold that the commoners were likely to behold adorned gilded chapels and the gleaming coats of arms of the royal and noble carriages.

"Riches do not profit in the day of wrath," warned Proverbs, and on All Saints' 1755 they didn't. Over the centuries Lisbon had grown sinfully flush on hostile trade, the exploitation of distant mines, and the traffic of human commodity, but when the disaster struck, like a biblical day of reckoning, most of what the city and its inhabitants had coveted was reduced to rubble, washed away, or turned to ash and scattered by the wind. But gone too was much that was loathsome. The Palácio da Inquisição was in ruins, along with two of its prisons; so too was the São Domingos Church, where the Inquisition read out its sentences and the friars incited the mob to pogroms. Medieval lanes, fetid and racked by disease, and the cramped houses that filled them lay buried. More important, an old absolutism had been shaken to its foundation. Lisbon, for all its religious self-consciousness and piety, had been forsaken. God had ceased to be just and nature to be beneficent. And while the city had much to mourn, the disaster would also usher in a new era, one in which a wholesome sense of doubt and the powers of reason would replace the certainties of religious dogma, and the numbing resignation that providence instilled would give way to the liberation of human promise.

In this sense, the earthquake could be construed not only as an irreparable tragedy but also as an opportunity of historic proportions. Certainly, Carvalho conceived of it as such. In *A Political Discourse on the Advantages Which the Kingdom of Portugal Can Obtain from the Misfortune Occasioned by the Memorable*

Earthquake of the 1ˢᵗ of November, 1755, the minister insisted not merely that disasters could be turned to a nation's advantage but that they were, in fact, necessary: "Politics is not always the cause of revolutions of State. Dreadful phenomena frequently change the face of Empires. One could say that these aberrations of nature are sometimes necessary because they can contribute more than anything to eradicating certain [antiquated] systems which are determined to invade the universal Empire . . . We could say that it is necessary that across the land provinces are wasted and cities ruined in order to dispel the blindness of certain nations, to enlighten them with the knowledge of their true interests. Yes, I dare say, in a certain sense, they [natural disasters] are necessary."[5] Needless to say, this was a sentiment that many Lisboans would have been hard pressed to share in the aftermath of the disaster, caught up as they were in personal tragedy and ruin, and unnerved by a thoroughly uncertain future; but by a cold and calculated reasoning, Carvalho was right. Lisbon would emerge from the ashes like a phoenix renewed and would cast off much of the obscurantism that had kept Portugal from beholding the light of a new age.

CHAPTER SIX

THE PREACHER AND THE PHILOSOPHER

Learn, O Lisbon, that the destroyers of our houses, palaces, churches, and convents, the cause of death of so many people and the flames that devoured vast treasures, are your abominable sins, and not comets, stars, vapors and exhalations, and similar natural phenomena.

—Father Gabriel Malagrida, *Juízo da verdadeira causa do terramoto*, 1756

All Nature is but Art, unknown to thee;
All Chance, Direction, which thou canst not see;
All Discord, Harmony not understood;
All partial Evil, universal Good:
And, spite of Pride, in erring Reason's spite,
One truth is clear, WHATEVER IS, IS RIGHT.

—Alexander Pope, *An Essay on Man*, 1733

N othing eased the moral consciences of the progressive minds of the Enlightenment quite as readily as Pope's relentless optimism. "Whatever is, is right" was the pronouncement of a deist convinced that God and his workings could be cast in a rational if impenetrable light. If the universe was the creation of a perfect, all-powerful God, then it must be the best of all possible worlds, went the seemingly flawless logic first put forth by Leibniz in 1710 in his *Essais de théodicée sur la bonté de Dieu, la liberté de l'homme, et l'origine du mal.* Human suffering, tragedy, the specter of war, famine, plague, and the catastrophes that nature unleashed were insignificant, a mere part of a divinely inspired whole that no one could ever hope to fully comprehend. By the light of reason, man should strive to decipher natural phenomena and human events; so armed, Good would logically triumph over Evil. Faith and reason would thus be reconciled. In 1733 a French critic reading Leibniz's *Théodicée* coined a new word to capture the spirit of the age: *optimisme.*

If there was a single event that cast irremediable doubt on such a Pollyanna philosophy, it was the Lisbon earthquake. Following the first report of the quake in the *Gazeta de Lisboa* on November 6, news of the disaster spread rapidly across Europe via coach and ship. The *Berlinische Nachrichten* reported the catastrophe on

November 11, the *Gazette de France* on November 22, the *London Magazine* and the Dutch *Graevenhaegse Courant* on November 26, and Copenhagen's *Kjobenhavns ridende Post* on December 5. Among the most noteworthy of these early reports of the disaster was one that appeared in the Parisian *Journal Étranger* in December. Written by Miguel Tibério Pedegache, a journalist, artist, and enlightened man of the times who moved in Carvalho's circle, the account was exceptional for its wealth of detail and the scientific bent of the narrative:

> On the 1st of November, 1755, with the barometer at 27 inches, 7 lines, the Reamur thermometer at 14 degrees above freezing, and with calm weather and clear skies, at 9:45 in the morning, the earth shook, but in such a weak manner that everyone imagined that it was nothing more than a carriage passing at high speed. This first tremor lasted two minutes. After an interval of two more minutes, the earth shook again, only with such violence that the majority of houses began to crack and roar. This second earthquake lasted approximately ten minutes. The dust raised was enough to obscure the sun. Again there was an interval of two or three minutes. As the thick dust settled, there was sufficient air and light for us to breathe and see around us. Then there came a shock so awful that the houses which had resisted the previous tremors collapsed with a crash. The sky again grew dark and the earth seemed to want to revert to chaos.

There wasn't a whiff of superstition or metaphysics in Pedegache's report, no ominous pronouncements about the wrath of

God, divine justice, providence, or sin, only the facts as best as he could explain them. Needless to say, this was just the sort of enlightened reporting that Carvalho needed in order to dispel Portugal's reputation for fanaticism and zealous religious exegeses, but as the weeks and months passed, the disaster sparked the eighteenth-century equivalent of a mass-media frenzy and the sobriety of the initial reports gave way to ever more lurid and sensational accounts.

"Perhaps the 'Daemon' of fear has never spread so rapidly and so powerfully its terror on earth," wrote Goethe.[1] Narratives grew more dramatic as the periodicals of the day heralded "new and accurate reports," "astonishing details," "real letters," and "firsthand accounts" by merchants, diplomats, churchmen, travelers, and seamen who had survived the destruction. In Great Britain, especially, the news had grown so persistent and detailed as to inspire incredulity. Asked if he believed the initial descriptions of the destruction of Lisbon, Samuel Johnson replied: "Oh! not for six months at least. I *did* think that story too dreadful to be credited, and can hardly yet persuade myself that it was true to the full extent we all of us have heard."[2]

The earthquake became the subject of commentaries, cautionary tales, speculation, and heated debate in churches, salons, universities, civil institutions, and the street. To complement the terror-fraught narratives of the disaster that were appearing in the press, images were soon included—mostly copperplate engravings—that brought home the tragedy with chilling if not always accurate detail. Most of the unsigned engravings, published in broadsheets all over Europe, especially England, France, Holland, and Germany, were churned out by sweatshop engravers in record time to satisfy the public appetite for a visual reference of a calamity that seemed to defy description. Rigor in rendering the architectural or natural landscape of Lisbon accurately counted for little. An image published in Bohemia in 1755, for example, depicted Lisbon's buildings in a decidedly Central European baroque style. But fidelity hardly mattered. It sufficed to show buildings in ruin, the river in a tempest, flames leaping, and crowds in utter panic to give the public—much of which was illiterate—a notion of the dimensions of the disaster.* Only the French engraver Jacques Philippe Le Bas (1707–83) took pains to give his work a measure of realism, but he had the distinct advantage of working from drawings created by the artists Paris and Pedegache, who were in Lisbon at the time of the earthquake.

Naturally, the collective reaction of the European public to these accounts and images of destruction was one of horror but also of puzzlement. To what divine plan could such an episode possibly belong? What benevolent God would bury thousands of innocent souls beneath ruins, stir up the sea to swallow bystanders, and spread an all-consuming fire, and to what end? Moreover, why would he do so in Lisbon, a city of such demonstrable religiosity and devotion? What could licentious Paris or avaricious London expect from the Almighty if pious Lisbon's fate had verged on the apocalyptic? Neither Leibniz nor Pope lived to hear news of the Lisbon quake, but their rosy precepts were dealt a mighty blow. If this was indeed the best of all possible worlds, what were the others? In *Dichtung und Wahrheit* Goethe recalled the effect that the news of the Lisbon disaster produced on him as a young boy of six in his native Frankfurt: "God, the Creator and

---

*The subject had a remarkable longevity. As late as the nineteenth and early twentieth centuries, engravings were still being commissioned to illustrate the disaster for a public that, then as now, showed a morbid attraction to catastrophe.

Upholder of Heaven and Earth, whom the explanation of the first article of the Creed declared to be so wise and merciful, insofar as He had abandoned the just and unjust to a like destruction, had in no way shown Himself to be fatherly. In vain did my young mind seek to fortify itself against such impressions. This was all the less possible as the wise men learned in the Scriptures could not agree as to the way in which such a phenomenon should be regarded."[3]

There was, however, one celebrated voice that the European royal courts and intellectual elites awaited with particular expectation, the voice of a playwright, poet, and philosopher who would no doubt shed the proper light on so controversial and bewildering an issue. They awaited Voltaire.

It took more than three weeks for the news of Lisbon's destruction to reach Voltaire at Les Délices, his country estate outside Geneva, where he was living a forced though exceedingly comfortable exile from Louis XV's France.* With his habitual perspicacity, Voltaire grasped at once the significance of the cataclysm and its repercussions for the prevailing philosophy of the times, as is clear from a letter that he wrote to his banker and financial adviser, Jean-Robert Tronchin, on November 24, a day after having received word of the disaster:

> This is indeed a cruel piece of natural philosophy! We shall find it difficult to discover how the laws of movement operate in such fearful disasters *in the best of all possible worlds*—where a hundred thousand ants,

---

*Louis XV forbade Voltaire to return to France after the philosopher accepted an appointment as chamberlain and poet-in-residence at the rival court of Frederick the Great of Prussia from 1750 to 1753.

our neighbours, are crushed in a second on our ant-
heaps, half dying undoubtedly in inexpressible agonies,
beneath debris from which it was impossible to extricate them, families all over Europe reduced to beggary,
and the fortunes of a hundred merchants—Swiss, like
yourself—swallowed up in the ruins of Lisbon. What a
game of chance human life is! What will the preachers
say—especially if the Palace of the Inquisition is left
standing! I flatter myself that those reverend fathers,
the Inquisitors, will have been crushed just like other
people. That ought to teach men not to persecute men:
for, while a few sanctimonious humbugs are burning
a few fanatics, the earth opens and swallows up all
alike.[4]

But Voltaire had discovered a subject that he urgently wished
to treat in more than mere correspondence, and by the beginning
of December he had composed his *Poème sur le désastre de Lisbonne* in 234 lines of exquisite Alexandrine verse. It was not, alas,
what his public had expected. In works such as the *Lettres phi-
losophiques sur les anglais* and *Discours en vers sur l'homme*, Voltaire
had shown a pronounced anticlerical streak; indeed he rarely
missed an opportunity to attack the Catholic Church for a host of
sins, from inveterate superstition to the murderous abuses of the
Inquisition, but for once he left the Church and religion almost
entirely aside and took aim instead at the philosophy of optimism
of Leibniz, Pope, and company. The poem, subtitled *An Inquiry
into the Maxim Whatever Is, Is Right*, also included a preface in
which Voltaire's growing pessimism took the form of another
maxim altogether more ancient and universal: "There is evil
upon the earth." The verses then plunged into the horror of the

earthquake and the feebleness of the philosophers' sanguine outlook:

> Oh wretched man, earth-fatal to be cursed
> Abyss of Plagues, and miseries the worst!
> Horrors on horrors, griefs on grief must show
> That man's the victim of unceasing woe,
> And lamentations which inspire my strain,
> Prove that philosophy is false and vain
>
> . . . .
>
> Seeing these stacks of victims, will you state,
> Vengeance is God's, they have deserved their fate?
> He is unshackled, tractable, and just.
> How comes he, to violate our trust.
>
> . . . .
>
> Say what advantage can result to all
> From Lisbon's lamentable fall?
>
> . . . .
>
> Leibnitz can't tell me from what secret cause
> In a world governed by the wisest laws
> Lasting disorders, woes that never end
> With our vain pleasures, real suffering blend.[5]

It was as bleak a poem as eighteenth-century readers could fathom, and in its original version Voltaire concluded the work with two lines that were positively existential in scope: "What is necessary, o mortals? Mortals it is necessary to suffer / To submit in silence, adore and die." Dismissing the notion of optimism in the wake of the Lisbon disaster was easy enough for Voltaire, but his rather dire alternative—to suffer, submit, adore, and die—was no alternative at all, but closer to a form of existential capitulation. Voltaire, it seems, realized as much and changed the final lines; the revised ending was less despairing, but only moderately so: "Defects and sorrow, ignorance and woe/Hope he omitted, man's sole bliss below."

Voltaire sent the poem to a number of friends and acquaintances, among them the philosopher Jean-Jacques Rousseau, who by coincidence was also living in Geneva. (Although born in the city, he had lived most of his life in France.) Rousseau may have been close to twenty years Voltaire's junior and not nearly so celebrated, but that did not prevent him from questioning the great man's attack on optimism. In a lengthy letter dated August 18, 1756, Rousseau, after some perfunctorily deferential remarks to the master, made it clear that his interpretation of the Lisbon crisis was radically different from that of Voltaire. Rousseau's argument was, in fact, one of the first to frame the disaster in a social scientific context.[6] "Without departing from your subject of Lisbon," wrote the author of the *Discours sur l'origine de l'inégalité parmi les hommes*, "admit, for example, that nature did not construct twenty thousand houses of six to seven stories there, and that if the inhabitants of this great city had been more equally spread out and more lightly lodged, the damage would have been much less and perhaps of no account."[7] Never mind that Rousseau appears to have been grossly misinformed about both the architectural composition of Lisbon, a city where seven-story buildings simply didn't exist, and about the destructive power of the earthquake itself. To suggest that the damage would have been "perhaps of no account" had the buildings been more spread out or lightly lodged was preposterous, as untold hundreds of victims were buried beneath the rubble of quite modest-size houses. According to Rousseau, much of the blame for the death toll was due to human folly. "How many unfortunate people have perished in this disaster because of one wanting to take his clothes, another his papers, another his money?"

Many of Rousseau's arguments, however were legitimate, and his perspective must have given Voltaire reason to reflect, as when he asked, "Should it be . . . that nature ought to be subjected to our laws, and that in order to interdict an earthquake, we have only to build a city there?" But at the close of the letter Rousseau suddenly turned to personal distinctions between the two philosophers, noting that Voltaire, acclaimed and rich, had become jaundiced and saw only evil in the world, while he, Rousseau, sought out all that was good, despite his humble circumstances and relative obscurity. "You enjoy," he taunted, "but I hope, and hope adorns everything."

Voltaire responded to this act of impertinence not by engaging in any philosophical jousting, which was clearly what the younger philosopher had hoped to initiate, but by making a well-crafted snub. On September 12 Voltaire wrote back to Rousseau: "My dear philosopher, we are able, you and I, in the intervals of our ills, to reason in verse and prose. But at the present moment, you will pardon me for leaving there all these philosophical discussions which are only amusements." In reality, Voltaire was merely putting off a nettlesome colleague (although it was he who had sent him the poem in the first place). His interest in the philosophical implications of the Lisbon earthquake was obviously more than an amusement, and he had more to say about the shallowness and perils of optimism than could be expressed in his *Poème*. But did Voltaire suspect, one cannot help but wonder, that the whole episode would prompt him to write his masterpiece?

In 1759 Voltaire published *Candide, ou l'optimisme* under the curious pseudonym of M. Le Docteur Ralph; the work, purportedly translated from the German, came out simultaneously in Paris, Geneva, and Amsterdam. Initially, authorities in Paris and

Geneva sought to suppress the book, and it is easy to see why. Although ostensibly a picaresque tale of international travel and adventure, the novel made scarcely concealed mockery of, among other things, the nobility, the military, the Church, the Inquisition, metaphysics, and above all Leibniz's optimism. The same qualities that inspired official disfavor, however, also made it an instant hit with the public, and authorities soon gave up on their attempts at censure. In its first year of publication alone *Candide* sold roughly thirty thousand copies and went through some twenty editions, including three in English and another in Italian. By eighteenth-century standards, the novel was an unequivocal blockbuster, and it brought Voltaire widespread public acclaim and not a little money. In time *Candide* would prove to be Voltaire's most enduring work and his indisputable masterpiece (today, indeed, it is difficult to cite any other of his works that are still read by the general public), and it exposed generations of readers to the physical and moral horrors of the Lisbon disaster.

Candide's universal appeal is hardly puzzling; it is a bawdy comic novel full of irreverence and violence that gleefully attacks conventional social and religious morals. It also unfolds at a whirlwind pace. Candide, the protagonist, is a bastard child who was brought up in the noble castle of Baron Thunder-ten-tronckh of Westphalia. Following an indiscretion with the baron's daughter, Candide is banished from the house and is soon joined by his old tutor, the philosopher Pangloss, who has always taught his charge, like Leibniz, that they live in the best of all worlds. They embark on a frenetic world tour of misadventure, in which they are submitted to every conceivable horror and humiliation, both natural and man-made, and along the way optimism is relentlessly assaulted by the grim realities of the world. Candide pops up in Holland, Cádiz, Buenos Aires, Paraguay, El Dorado, Surinam,

Paris, Portsmouth, Venice, Constantinople, and of course Lisbon, where his arrival coincides with the earthquake, and where he soon finds himself half-buried in the rubble:

> Candide had been hurt by some falling rocks; he lay in the street covered with debris. He said to Pangloss: "Alas! Get me a little wine and oil; I am dying."
>
> "This earthquake is not a new thing," replied Pangloss. "The town of Lima felt the same shock in America last year; similar causes produce similar effects; there must certainly be a train of sulphur underground from Lima to Lisbon."
>
> "Nothing is more probable," replied Candide; "but, for God's sake, a little oil and wine."
>
> "What do you mean probable?" replied the philosopher; "I maintain that it is proved."[8]

Candide, in his inimitable way, always manages to escape or to survive his predicaments, and the earthquake is no exception, but no sooner has he recovered from the ordeal than he finds himself and Pangloss prisoners of the Inquisition for the blasphemous crime of having questioned the doctrines of original sin and free will:

> After the earthquake which destroyed three-quarters of Lisbon, the wise men of that country could discover no more efficacious way of preventing total ruin than by giving the people a splendid *auto-da-fé*. It was decided by the university of Coimbra that the sight of several persons being slowly burned in great ceremony is an infallible secret for preventing earthquakes.[9]

Candide and Pangloss, of course, are to be the victims, along with a Biscayan who had married his godmother, and "two Portuguese who, when eating a chicken, had thrown away the bacon." (This last piece of "evidence" was presumed to be the act of crypto-Jews.) When the appointed day arrives,

> They marched in procession and listened to a most pathetic sermon, followed by lovely plain song music. Candide was flogged in time to the music, while the singing went on; the Biscayan and the two men who had not wanted to eat the bacon were burned, and Pangloss was hanged, although this is not the usual practice. The very same day, the earth shook again with a terrible clamor.
>
> Candide, terrified, dumbfounded, bewildered, covered with blood, quivering from head to foot, said to himself: "If this is the best of all possible worlds, what are the others?"[10]

The question was as close to metaphysics as Voltaire would come. With *Candide* the poet had effectively buried *optimisme* and exposed it for the naïve and witless tenet that it was. Before long a new word was coined that arose frequently in the public vocabulary, *Panglossian*, which *Webster's* defines as "naively or blindly optimistic."

Still, Voltaire's satire failed to provide a compelling alternative. He struggled with the novel's conclusion just as he had with the final lines of his *Poème*, and the result was a concluding note not so much of desperation as of resignation. Candide, Pangloss (he survives the gallows), and a band of fellow travelers end up on a farm on the fertile shores of the Marmona Sea in Asia Minor, where they work the land and find contentment. In the novel's final passage, the incorrigible Pangloss offers Candide one last observation:

> "All events are linked up in this best of all possible worlds; for, if you had not been expelled from the noble castle, by hard kicks on your behind for the love of Mademoiselle Cunégonde, if you had not been clapped into the Inquisition, if you had not wandered about America on foot, if you had not stuck your sword in the Baron, if you had not lost all your sheep from the land of Eldorado, you would not be here eating candied citrons and pistachios."
>
> " 'Tis well said," replied Candide, "but we must cultivate our gardens."[11]

The cultivation of the garden was an apt metaphor for engaging in simple, down-to-earth work for which one could expect to reap modest but fruitful rewards. It was a deceptively simple piece of advice from a poet who had discovered as much at Les Délices, but as a consolation for the victims of a natural disaster like the Lisbon earthquake or a man-made evil like the tribunals of the Inquisition, the utterance fell exasperatingly short. Nevertheless, *Candide* helped to jar the complacency of an age faced with manifest horror (and never more so than in Lisbon); it certainly marked a turning point for Voltaire. Gone were the courtly histories, plays, and poems that had curried so much favor with the establishment; henceforth Voltaire's literary voice grew more popular and his conscience increasingly concerned with human justice and the plight of the common man. It was as if Europe's most worldly man of letters had suddenly discovered the world.

Philosophers may have wrangled over the nature and cause of the Lisbon disaster, but for the city's legion of clergy there had never been a doubt and even less vacillation. Their reaction was as predictable as it was hoary—the earthquake was a divine act of reckoning for a city steeped in sin. Before the tremors had even subsided, priests were exhorting the panic-stricken crowds to repent and were admonishing the survivors for a litany of sins, including avarice, loose morals, sloth, corruption, and a tepid faith that submitted to heretics, that is to say Protestants, in their midst!

The most vehement voice amid this general rant belonged to Father Gabriel Malagrida, an Italian Jesuit who had a wide following in Lisbon as a mystic and missionary, and who had counted the late João V among his most fervid advocates. Malagrida was born in Menaggio, Italy; he joined the Society of Jesus in Genoa; and in 1721 he sailed from Lisbon to Brazil to preach the Gospel and convert the heathen. He stayed for nearly thirty years, battling hostile natives, disease, and the torpor of the topics, and his reputation as a saintlike figure spread throughout Latin America and eventually back to Portugal. It was João V who had Malagrida recalled to Lisbon in 1749; the king was ailing, and despite having wrenched the title of *Fidelissimus* from the papacy, built the glory that was Mafra, and heaped gold and luxury on the Church, he sought an extraordinary absolution from the renowned missionary. When Malagrida was ushered before the king at court, João V placed the Jesuit's hands on his own head. "Bless the king, thy servant," murmured Malagrida, looking heavenward. "Do not call me king, call me sinner," João replied.

The royal patronage only added to Malagrida's mystique, and he remained in Lisbon as confessor to João V and, after the king's death in 1750, to the powerful Távora family. He wielded enormous influence at court, and in the years leading up to the Lisbon earthquake Malagrida came into open conflict with the new secretary of state, Sebastião José de Carvalho e Melo, who was determined to curb ecclesiastical power, especially that of the Society of Jesus. In 1751 Carvalho had managed to make all sentences passed by the Inquisition subject to revision by the Crown, a breach of Church prerogative that won the secretary of state the general enmity of the clergy. But it was Carvalho's effort to wrest administrative control of the Brazilian missions from the Jesuits that transformed Malagrida into his most vocal and dangerous enemy.

Now, in the chaotic aftermath of the quake, Carvalho needed the support of the Church. But there was scarcely a man of the cloth to whom he could turn, and those whom he could still count as friends, like the Oratorian António Pereira de Figueireda, lacked the ecclesiastical clout to marshal the Church in Carvalho's favor. Rather than preaching uplifting sermons and taking an active part in Lisbon's restoration, as Carvalho had hoped, the priesthood was mostly coaxing survivors to repent and recommending prayer retreats to assuage the disaster. Malagrida had delivered a series of incendiary sermons to his growing legion of followers that were soon published in an inopportune pamphlet entitled *Juízo da verdadeira causa do terramoto* (An Opinion on the True Cause of the Earthquake). Malagrida's style, honed at the Jesuit seminary and inflamed by decades in the tropics, was, if anything, brutally unambiguous:

> Tragic Lisbon is now a mound of ruins. Would that it were less difficult to think of some method of restoring the place; but it has been abandoned, and the refugees of the city live in despair. As for the dead, what a great harvest of sinful souls such disasters send to Hell! It is scandalous to pretend the earthquake was just a

natural event, for if that be true, there is no need to repent and try to avert the wrath of God, and not even
the Devil himself could invent a false idea more likely
to lead us all to irreparable ruin. Holy people had
prophesied that an earthquake was coming, yet the
city continued in its sinful ways without a care for the
future. Now, indeed, the case of Lisbon is desperate. It
is necessary to devote all our strength and purpose to
the task of repentance. Would to God we could see as
much determination and fervor for this necessary exercise as are devoted to the erection of huts and new
buildings! Does being billeted in the country outside
the city area put us outside the jurisdiction of God?
God undoubtedly desires to exercise His love and
mercy, but be sure that wherever we are, He is watch-
ing us, scourge in hand.[12]

In truth, this sort of fire-and-brimstone rhetoric was hardly exclusive to Portugal or even to the Catholic world at large. Indeed,
the association of disaster with divine punishment was as old as
man. Even an eighteenth century sown with the seeds of enlightenment perceived the hand of God to be behind catastrophes both
natural and human. Calvinist *predikants* in the Netherlands re-
verted to similar language when explaining the great flood of 1740
as an act of divine justice in which water would wash away the
filth and sin and bring the wicked to repentance. Nor was England
exempt from this sort of disaster-fed fanaticism. When the news
of Lisbon's destruction reached Britain, there was a widespread
fear that London, conspicuously more corrupt, avaricious, prone
to gambling, and licentious than the Portuguese capital, might
well be next. A member of Parliament actually proposed an urgent

return to the teachings of Moses as a means to avert the wrath of a righteous God. George II didn't go quite so far, but he did issue a royal decree proclaiming February 6, 1756, a day of fasting and penance throughout the British Isles.

Throughout Europe similar calls to prayer for Lisbon issued forth from cathedral pulpits and monasteries, parish churches and episcopal palaces, and, most generously perhaps, the odd synagogue. In Hamburg, where several hundred Portuguese Jews lived in exile, the governors of the Sephardic synagogue circulated a pamphlet on March 11, 1756, ordering a day of fasting in order to pray and beg for mercy from the Divine Majesty for the destruction unleashed in Lisbon. These collective prayers were welcome enough, but to mock the recovery efforts and the building of shelters for the refugees, as Malagrida had done, was something bordering on the treasonous. A city consumed exclusively with its own repentance was a city doomed. "They [Lisboans] thought it almost impious for them to endeavour to take care of themselves," observed the British merchant Thomas Chase, "and many of them called it 'fighting against Heaven!'"[13]

Carvalho needed an energized populace that was committed to rebuilding, and he was having difficulty finding it with the likes of Malagrida terrorizing the scattered and forlorn flock with sermons of God's retribution. Carvalho first protested to the Lisbon patriarch, but José Cardinal Manuel da Câmara d'Atalaia was little disposed to censure a figure with so a saintly an aura as Malagrida; furthermore, he admired him for his zeal. The minister, infuriated, took his petition directly to the king and, for good measure, to the papal nuncio as well. José I was reluctant to silence the man who had provided spiritual solace to his father, João V, in the final days of his long reign, but he was even less inclined to deny support to Carvalho, the one man who was willing to go to any length to resurrect his capital and preserve his throne. In the autumn of 1756, shortly after the publication of his *An Opinion on the True Cause of the Earthquake*, Malagrida was sent into internal exile in Setúbal and forbidden to preach about the earthquake; he was, however, far from finished; he had his avid following, powerful friends such as the Távora family, and the hard-won, unyielding faith of a born missionary. The minister and the missionary would clash again in the years to come, although with altogether more conclusive results.

The sermons of woe were hardly confined to the Catholic pulpits. In Protestant countries throughout Europe but especially in Britain, which had suffered considerable human, material, and economic loss in Lisbon, the subject of the earthquake was persistently alluded to in Sunday sermons, although the focus of the vicars and divines was utterly distinct from that of their Catholic counterparts. To the Protestant conscience, God had unleashed His vengeance on Lisbon for its popish idolatry and for the sins on the bloodstained hands of the Inquisition and all its agents. A visceral anti-Catholic prejudice was nothing new; on the contrary, it had been nurtured in the British Isles and throughout Protestant Europe since the Reformation, but the Lisbon earthquake provided the ideal stage on which to play out the apocalyptic drama of Judgment Day, and there was little doubt as to the role of the damned.

No Protestant preacher articulated this sentiment quite as forcefully as John Wesley (1703–91), the founder of Methodism and a visionary social crusader. Just weeks after the earthquake Wesley published a tract entitled *Serious Thoughts Occasioned by the Late Earthquake at Lisbon*, which sought to put the disaster in a proper theological perspective for a British public alarmed by the tragedy. In the zeal of his exposition, Wesley was every bit Malagrida's equal:

And what shall we say of the late accounts from Portugal? That several thousand houses, and many thousand persons are no more. That a fair city is now in ruinous heaps? Is there indeed a God that judges the world? And is he now making inquisition for blood? If so, it is not surprising, he should begin there, where so much blood has been poured on the ground like water, where so many brave men have been murdered in the most base and cowardly as well as barbarous manner, almost every day, as well as every night, while none regarded or laid it to heart. How long has their blood been crying from the earth? Yea, how long has the bloody House of Mercy, the title which the Inquisition in Portugal takes to itself, the scandal not only of all religions, but even of human nature, stood to insult both Heaven and Earth! And shall I not visit for these things, saith the Lord? Shall not my soul be avenged on such a city as this?[14]

And just in case anyone might have missed or ignored the book, Wesley converted the message to the hymnal:

> Woe! To the Men on Earth who dwell,
> Nor dread th'Almighty Frown,
> When God doth all his Wrath reveal,
> And showers his Judgments down!
> Sinners, expect those heaviest Showers,
> To meet your God prepare,
> When lo! The Seventh Angel pours
> His Vial in the Air!
> Or
> Awake, ye guilty Souls, awake,

Nor sleep, till Tophet takes you in!
The Lord of Hosts is ris'n to shake,
The Earth polluted with your Sin.[15]

The fervor with which Wesley worked the theme of Lisbon's destruction and the horror he struck in his readers and listeners were not to the liking of all Protestants, particularly the more subdued Anglicans, who tended to shrink from sermons that used fear as a path to conversion. "The author, in my opinion, with good parts and learning, is a most dark and saturnine creature," wrote Thomas Herring, archbishop of Canterbury, in a letter to a friend regarding Wesley's *Serious Thoughts*. "His picture may frighten weak people, that, at the same time, are wicked, but I fear he will make few converts, except for a day. I read his Serious Thoughts, but, for my own part, I think the rising and the setting of the sun is a more durable argument for religion than all the extraordinary convulsions of nature put together."[16] Still, the habitual Anglican moderation aside, a large portion of Protestant Europe, nurtured as it was on anti-Catholic propaganda and the Black Legend, tended to regard Lisbon's chastisement as somehow deserved, as well as a timely opportunity to cast off superstition and accept the true light of the reformed faith. This theme of disaster as a means to spiritual awakening was at the heart of Frans de Haes's epic poem *Het verheerlykte en vernederde Portugal* (Portugal Glorified and Humiliated), perhaps the most important Dutch literary work to emerge from the disaster. Before Lisbon can be reborn, the poem says, the city must first dispel darkness, mists, and vapors:

But please it you, oh Lord, to first and foremost enlighten
    spirit.
Chase those mists, with which Idolatry,

Sinful Superstition, and cruel Tyranny
So pitifully blind, alas, the Soul's Eye,
That Religion there is called the shackling of Man's
free conscience.
Banish that hellish vapour, that thick darkness,
So that they may recognize how beautifully shines the
Savior Sun,
Whose fire of love teaches us to love you first, with our soul
and our senses,
And next our neighbours, like as ourselves.
This way Portugal, through your all wise direction
And favours unearned, may be reformed for eternity.[17]

Wesley's and de Haes's words would never have reached the
ears of the average Portuguese; nor would they have caused him
much concern if they had, coming as they did from heretics. The
Catholic Church and the Portuguese faithful attributed the error
of the Inquisition not to its murderous excesses; quite the contrary. The Santo Oficio, they insisted, had been too lax with of-
fenders of the faith and not relentless enough in rooting out
dissenters, Judaizers, and heretics. Few could help but notice,
however, that the earthquake's destruction had taken a highly selective toll on the Inquisition. The Church of São Domingos,
where the Inquisition read out its sentences, had been burned
out; two of the Inquisition's principal prisons, whose torture
chambers were equipped with rack, wheel, and braziers, were destroyed; and the magnificent Palácio dos Estaus, which housed
the Tribunal do Santo Oficio, had collapsed, burying Lisbon's inquisitor general, Manuel Varejão de Távora, beneath the marble
debris. Lisbon's British residents celebrated this blow to Catholic
barbarity, at least among their own, and pointed out with undue

righteousness that their modest church and graveyard in the British Factory compound had survived the quake unscathed.

For all their doctrinal differences and their contrary readings of the disaster, however, staunch Protestants and Catholics agreed on one indisputable point: behind the earthquake lay the hand of God, and any talk of "natural" causes was akin to blasphemy. Anyone who did entertain a scientific approach to natural events was obliged to tread carefully. In the first months after the quake Carvalho had urged José Alvares da Silva, a scientifically minded Lisbon doctor, to write a pamphlet explaining the earthquake as a natural phenomenon, in response to the moral interpretations that were spewing from Lisbon's clergy. The result, entitled *Investigação das causes proximas do terramoto, succedido em Lisboa*, was enough to infuriate the likes of Malagrida, even if it was perhaps less forceful than Carvalho had hoped. The author invoked Francis Bacon as the inventor of the natural sciences and urged the Portuguese "to study experimental physics seriously and discover what natural forces can perform," but he was unwilling or unable to dismiss the possibility of a metaphysical cause. God, he admitted, may very well have caused the catastrophe. The Spanish theologians José de Cevallos and Benito Jerónimo Feijoo y Montenegro defended the earthquake as a natural occurrence but never dared to extricate God altogether from the scheme. "The earthquake has been entirely natural," wrote Cevallos in an introduction to Feijoo's *Nuevo systhema sobre la causa physica de los terremotos*, "caused by natural and proportional second causes, in which God partakes as in any other natural event."[18]

These early proponents of natural causes seemed to hedge their bets, as if they had one eye on the future and another on the Inquisition. Men, after all, had been burned for less. Yet these quasi-scientific responses to the earthquake that also bowed to religious

interpretation often came from places where the Inquisition held
no sway. A tack similar to that of Feijoo and Cevallos, for example,
was taken by the Reverend John Rogers, a minister in Leominster,
Massachusetts, who, moved by the destruction of Lisbon and
personally shaken by a mild quake that struck New England on
November 18, 1755, preached extensively on the causes and con-
sequences of earthquakes. That a Massachusetts minister was informed of Lisbon's fate (the news would have arrived first at Boston
harbor) and chose to make the disaster a recurrent theme of his
sermons is yet another indication of the international impact of
the quake. What Rogers expounded to the flock in Leominster,
and later published in Boston in 1756 as "The Terribility, and the
Moral Philosophy of Earthquakes," was that a phenomenon such
as an earthquake may well be attributed to natural causes—"that
they are not properly miraculous or preternatural, there seems to
be a very great Probability"—but that ultimately Nature was the
manifestation of the Divine Will.[19] He also cited a string of sins,
including "Acts of Irreligion, Avarice, Pride, Prodigality and Luxury,
Injustice, Falshood [sic], Deceit, Maligrity, Extortion, &c.," that were
sufficiently grievous to prompt an earthquake.[20] Curiously, most of
the sins he named were decidedly venal rather than mortal. For
Rogers, an earthquake was above all an opportunity for repentance, and its immediate purpose was to "make the Inhabitants of
the earth tremble . . . so that hereby they may be brought to a sense
of their Folly."[21] The folly of the Portuguese, according to Rogers as
well as John Wesley and most other Protestants, was their devotion
to idolatry; God's fury, however, could just as well be unleashed in
Massachusetts as in Lisbon:

> When God ariseth to shake terribly the Earth, all
> the rational Inhabitants, who know of it, (whether

they immediately hear and feel it, or not) should cast
away their Idols . . . Suppose ye that the Inhabitants of
Cadiz and *Lisbon* were greater Sinners than any other
of the Europeans whom God sparred from the earthquake? Probably no; or—greater than even the Protestants in America? (who have the Bible in their Hands,
but despise it)—possibly no. For those miserable Slaves
were not much better instructed than the very Pagan
Idolaters.*[22]

In Portugal, Malagrida's opinion that "not even the devil could
invent a false idea [natural causes] so liable to lead us to irreparable ruin" received the greatest credence. Indeed, it is hard to
imagine where anyone in Portugal would have gone to draw on
the sort of enlightened thought that would inspire a more scientific grasp of natural events. Paradoxically, new ideas were sometimes sequestered in the more progressive religious orders inside
the Church itself. In Lisbon, for example, the Oratorians' library
included works by Francis Bacon, John Locke, René Descartes,
and Antonio Genovesi, and the Convento das Necessidades even
had a laboratory devoted to the natural sciences, but these were
hermetic religious orders where the public never entered. The
more cosmopolitan nobles, like the Marquês de Louriçal, had private libraries, but these were the exclusive domains of the titled
elite.

Nor would conventional schooling have introduced students
to the intellectual advances of the age. By the mid-eighteenth
century the Jesuits had had a grip on national education for two

---

*It is worth noting that John Rogers, a kind of proto-Unitarian, was driven from
his Leominster church in 1758 for his unorthodox views, which included questioning the divinity of Christ.

hundred years, and they maintained a syllabus that was painfully archaic. The University of Coimbra, the country's paradigm of higher learning, banned all scientific works and did not even offer studies in the natural sciences. In order to keep modern works written in vernacular languages at bay, the educational program still used Latin exclusively. In 1746 the dean of the Coimbra College of Arts issued a chilling decree forbidding "any conclusions contrary to the Aristotelian system," especially, he emphasized, "new opinions, rarely accepted or useless for the study of the Major Sciences, such as those of René Descartes, Gassendi, Newton and others."[23] Students of the earthquake would have learned from Aristotle that it had something vaguely to do with subterranean winds and fire, but Catholic theologians recast even this protoscientific explanation—Aristotle's underground fires simply became Hell.

Such religious obscurantism, needless to say, had a decidedly deadening effect on the Portuguese's power of inquiry. Just as the rest of Europe was heady with scientific discoveries and debate, Portugal and neighboring Spain, the bastions of arch-Catholic orthodoxy, were trapped in a medieval world dominated by ecclesiastics and shackled by dogma. The tenor of the times was rather bluntly expressed by a Spanish Dominican friar, who wrote, "We prefer to be mistaken with St. Basil and St. Augustine than to be correct with Descartes and Newton."[24]

Among the few Portuguese infused with an enlightened spirit of the times were the so-called Estrangeirados ("foreignized" Portuguese who had worked or had been educated abroad), a circle that included diplomats, international merchants, and a goodly number of "New Christians" whose families had opted for exile when the climate of religious persecution grew too stifling. Carvalho, having lived in both London and Vienna, was a member of this urbane caste. So were the "New Christian" physician and Encyclopedist António Ribeiro Sanches, whom Carvalho had met in Vienna; the Hungarian-born architect and engineer Carlos Mardel, who had served João V as court architect; and Luís António Verney, the author of the 1746 *Verdadeiro método de estudar* (True Method of Study). The informal group had diverse interests that ran from architecture and economics to education and the natural sciences, but they all shared a cultural outlook acquired abroad that the home-bound Portuguese conspicuously lacked.

The Estangeirados had read Colbert on economic and financial reform; Bacon, Hume, and Locke on empirical methods; Descartes on metaphysics; and Newton on natural philosophy. They rejected moral and supernatural explanations for the earthquake and looked to natural phenomena and the scientific method as a means of deciphering the event; but they were an insignificant minority and, with the exception of Carvalho, largely powerless. The group was flush with new ideas and plans of reform for Portugal, but they faced a well-entrenched adversary in the Church. The Jesuits kept such enlightened minds out of the universities, where they might have instilled a generation of future leaders with the regenerative spirit of science and humanism, and the Inquisition kept them mostly silent by censuring the publication of any original scientific works and threatening to charge as heresy any whiff of a theory judged too iconoclastic. In Portugal, devotion to Descartes and Newton came at a frightful price.

Meanwhile, elsewhere in Europe, the Lisbon earthquake set off a flurry of scientific inquiry. In Königsberg, in the year following the disaster, Immanuel Kant published three tracts on earthquakes, regarding the event as a scientific rather than a moral phenomenon. In *History and Natural Descriptions of the noteworthy events of the*

Earthquake which shook at the end of the 1755th year large parts of the Earth (1756) Kant wrote: "If humans are building on inflammable material, over a short time the whole splendour of their edifices will be falling down by shaking. However, is this reason to blame providence for it?" The philosopher had his metaphysics straight, but his seismic speculations had not advanced much beyond the Aristotelian model of labyrinthine subterranean passageways fraught with wind and fire, which had been the generally accepted theory for two millennia. "The earthquakes reveal to us that the earth is full of vaults and cavities, and that beneath our feet hidden mines with various labyrinths run everywhere," Kant postulated. "All these cavities contain a glowing fire, or some combustible matter that requires but a small stimulation in order to rage with violence around it and to shake or even split the earth above it."

Kant's and Aristotle's hypotheses lacked an understanding of wave propagation that would have explained the effect and extent of seismic activity. The phenomenon of movement of geological faults that is the origin of earthquakes would take more than another century to discover, but their inability to conceive of movement in the earth from a seismic epicenter was a fundamental flaw. By the time of the Lisbon earthquake, the basis for a theory of wave propagation already existed. The English experimental philosopher Robert Hooke had touched upon the nature of elasticity in solids in the late seventeenth century, and in 1747 the French mathematician Jean le Rond d'Alembert solved the problem of wave motion in his experiments on the transverse vibrations of a uniform tense chord. In order to advance the fledgling field of seismology, however, someone had to connect the dots, and the Lisbon quake provided the impetus to do so.

The definitive breakthrough was made by the Reverend John Michell, a professor of geology and mineralogy at Cambridge, whose interest was piqued by the graphic eyewitness accounts of the Lisbon disaster that appeared prominently in the British press, including *The London Gazette, The Public Advertiser,* and *The Gentleman's Magazine.* For the first time European scientists, or "natural philosophers," had access to fairly reliable reports from the scene of a nearby disaster, in record time. And it does not seem too far-fetched to suppose that Michell's perusing of the press, in which Lisbon survivors referred repeatedly to the ground undulating like sea waves or windblown fields of wheat, may well have struck a eureka-like chord. Be that as it may, it was Michell who first articulated the wavelike nature of seismic activity in his groundbreaking essay *Conjectures concerning the Cause of Observations upon the Phaenomena of Earthquakes* (1760), in which he wrote: "The motion of the earth in earthquakes is partly tremulous, and partly propagated by waves which succeed one another sometimes at large and sometimes at small distances; and this latter motion is generally propagated much farther than the former." The analogy that Michell employed to illustrate the phenomenon to the layman was as commonplace as it was irrefutable: "Suppose a large cloth or carpet (spread upon a floor), to be raised at one edge, and then suddenly brought down again to the floor; the air under it, being by this means propelled, will pass along, till it escapes at the opposite side, raising the cloth in a wave all the way as it goes." A century later Robert Mallet would develop a far more comprehensive analysis of seismic disturbances, as a result of his study of the Neapolitan earthquake of 1857, but it is Michell and his speculation on the Lisbon disaster that effectively marks the birth of modern seismology.

It would be a mistake, however, to portray all of the Portuguese attitudes and observations regarding the earthquake as moralistic and immobile, and those elsewhere in Europe as wholly empirical and divorced from religion. The reality was far less clear-cut.

Mid-eighteenth-century Britain, for example, was undeniably a place of extraordinary scientific and technological advancement, the birthplace of Newton and Halley, Hume and Maclaurin; but the spirit of the age was by no means universally embraced. A scriptural interpretation of natural and human-inspired events had a long and resilient history. Among the popular rumors for the cause of the Great London Fire of 1666, for instance, was said to be God's displeasure with Charles II for having taken a Catholic wife, the Portuguese Catarina de Bragança. And a series of mild earthquakes in England in 1750 gave rise to the widespread notion that the end was at hand, causing a spiritual revival throughout the country. Nor did the average British subject regard the Lisbon quake as a purely natural event—far from it. John Michell and his scientifically like-minded contemporaries may have been engaging in rigorous empiricism, but to the man in the street, the scourge-wielding hand of God still had more resonance as an explanation for catastrophe. These were the souls who flocked in droves to hear the preaching of John Wesley or George Whitefield, and it wasn't budding science that they got, but a thunderous dose of the good, old-time religion. Wesley's take on natural causes for physical phenomena was as obstinate as anything the Catholic theologians could come up with:

> The Earth threatens to swallow you up. Where is your Protection now? . . . If anything can help, it must be Prayer. But what will thou pray to? Not to the God of Heaven: you suppose him to have nothing to do with Earthquakes. No: they proceed in a merely natural Way, either from the Earth itself, or from included Air, or from subterranean Fires or Water. If thou prayest then (which perhaps thou never didst before) it

must be to some of these. Begin. "O Earth, Earth, Earth, hear the Voice of thy Children. Here, O Air, Water, Fire!" And will you hear? You know, it cannot be. How deplorable then is this Condition, who in such an Hour has None else to flee to? How uncomfortable the Supposition which implies this, by direct, necessary Consequence, namely, that all these Things are the pure Result of merely Natural Causes![25]

In fact, the supposition of natural causes provided considerably more comfort. Science transformed the religious zealot's sinners into mere victims of a natural disaster; guilt was replaced by happenstance, and the call to repentance by the imperative of rebuilding and renewal. If religious dogma was capable of making survivors cower with the threat of damnation and the promise of redemption, science could reveal the mechanics of the natural world and liberate the ignorant and credulous from centuries of fanaticism. Carvalho, along with other Estrangeirados and the odd enlightened mind, knew this and was determined that in the dialectic over the interpretation of the calamity, the light of reason should triumph over religious obscurantism. So while Malagrida and his like were in the streets preaching repentance and the futility of rebuilding, Carvalho searched for the rational principles that would explain a natural cataclysm to a populace that had hitherto been educated from the pulpit.

In January 1756 Carvalho published a survey of thirteen questions, a kind of seismological questionnaire, which was sent to the diocese throughout Portugal. Carvalho himself probably did not actually compose the questions; more likely they were the work of Sanches or Verney. But Carvalho sponsored the initiative that would become known to history as the Pombal Survey, one of the foundational documents of modern seismology. The questions attempted to frame the parameters of the disaster along purely scientific lines; they are virtually the same questions that any conscientious contemporary seismologist would pose, without the benefit of modern instruments of calibration:

I: At what time did the earthquake begin on November 1 and how long did it last?

II: Did you perceive the shock to be greater from one direction than another? Example: From north to south, or to the contrary, did buildings seem to fall more to one side than another?

III: How many buildings were ruined in each parish, were there notable buildings among them, and in what state did they remain?

IV: How many people died, [and] were any of them distinguished?

V: Did you notice what happened to the sea, to fountains, and to rivers?

VI: Did the sea rise or fall first, and how many hands did it rise above normal, how many times did you notice the extraordinary rise or fall, and did you notice how long it took to fall and to rise?

VII: Did any fissures appear in the earth, what did you notice about them, and did any new spring appear?

VIII: What measures were immediately taken in each place by the priests, the army, and the ministers?

IX: Did any earthquakes occur after that of November 1, when, and what damage did they cause?

X: Have there been any other earthquakes in living memory, and what damage did they cause?

XI: How many people live in each parish, and declare, as
   far as possible, how many of each sex there are?
XII: Has there been any shortage of food?
XIII: If fire broke out, how long did it last, and what damages did it cause?

These questions may well appear startlingly routine today, but
for eighteenth-century Portugal, they were nothing short of revolutionary in their objectivity. Absent was any allusion to metaphysics or morals; they made no reference to omens or sinful
deeds, no mention of God or divine wrath. Some were poignant
questions regarding the actions and effects of the earthquake,
while others clearly displayed a concern for modern disaster management, inquiring about the measures adopted by the authorities or the state of food supplies. Not only had God been left out
of the picture, but an enlightened state had stepped to the fore.

CHAPTER SEVEN

LIKE A PHOENIX FROM THE FLAMES

As the houses, convents, churches, etc., are large, and all built with white stone, they look very beautiful at a distance; but as you approach nearer, and find them to want every kind of ornament, all idea of beauty vanishes at once . . . If a man was suddenly to be removed from Palmyra hither, and should take a view of no other city, in how glorious light would the ancient architecture appear to him! And what desolation and destruction of arts and sciences would he conclude had happened between the several eras of these cities!

—Henry Fielding, *Journal of a Voyage to Lisbon*, 1755

Fielding was one of the last foreign observers to leave a literary reference to Lisbon before the fall. His habitually critical eye may have been accentuated on account of his physical condition; he was dying of jaundice and dropsy. The author of the inimitable novel *The History of Tom Jones, a Foundling* (1749) had arrived in Lisbon in August 1754, with his wife and a daughter, seeking warmer climes for his deteriorating health; but neither Fielding nor his doctors were under any illusions about the time left to him. The journey from England had been long and tedious, a record of which appears in the posthumous *Journal of a Voyage to Lisbon*, one of the great works on the horrors of travel. What Fielding had to say about Lisbon wasn't kind. He duly admired the Jerónimos Monastery and the expansive vistas of the Tagus, but he dismissed the capital itself, even viewed from the relative comfort of a sedan chair, as "the nastiest city in the world." Nor, it seems, did the change of climate do him much good. He died on October 8, scarcely two months after his arrival, and was buried in the English cemetery. A stone monument, erected in 1830, bears the inscription *Luget Britannia gremio non dari fovere natum* (Britannia laments not having healed her son at her bosom).

As jaundiced as Fielding was feeling, however, he wasn't entirely off the mark. True, Lisbon had its share of splendid palaces and gilt-filled churches, and the Tagus and the city's seven hills lent it a singular topographical beauty; but by the mid-eighteenth century the general air of the capital had become ramshackle and unwholesome. The medieval streets and alleys were twisted and irregularly paved, sullied by open sewers and frequently unfit for carriage traffic. The justly famous white stone of Lisbon was the building material of choice for palaces, churches, and finer houses, but the majority of tenements, crowded and built oppressively close, were made of mere adobe. In the Baixa quarter, the city's historic center, flooding from the Tagus, vermin, and epidemics were common. There were few public spaces of note, except perhaps the Rossio square, where the well-to-do gathered to promenade, jockey in their sedan chairs, and gossip, but only in the light of day. Venturing out after nightfall unarmed was considered madness.

Quitting Lisbon's center in the aftermath of the quake would have been understandable enough; the Baixa had been leveled and thoroughly burned out, and thousands of corpses remained buried in the debris. "They [the populace] have been employed for several days last past, in taking up the dead bodies," wrote an English merchant on November 18, "which are carried out into the neighboring fields, but the greater part still remains under the rubbish, nor do I think 'twould be safe to remove them tho' it were practicable on account of the stench. The King they say, talks of building a new city at Belém. But be this as it will, 'tis certain he will have no thoughts of rebuilding the old, until these bodies have lain long enough to be consumed."[1] The general opinion was that Lisbon had been dealt its deathblow and that to attempt to rebuild the city was only to tempt God (said the pious) or Nature (said the philosophers). But while both dogma and reason may have dictated abandoning Lisbon to its stricken fate, powerful historic and social ties to the capital weren't easily severed. The Baixa had been settled since ancient times; like Portugal itself, it was a veritable palimpsest of Phoenician, Carthaginian, Roman, Visigoth, Moorish, and Christian culture. The quarter housed many of the country's most emblematic royal, ecclesiastic, commercial, and cultural institutions and comprised a geography of power and national identity. The Paço da Ribeira, the waterfront palace built by Manuel I in the early sixteenth century, was the seat of the monarchy and the patriotic scene of the restoration of Portuguese independence from Spain. In the shadows of the palace lay quays and the Casa da India, where the fruits and spoils of a far-flung empire arrived to embellish a capital with oriental splendor. The quarter featured monuments to charity like the Hospital de Todos os Santos, which had offered relief to the sick and destitute since the late fifteenth century, as well as monuments to unspeakable cruelty, like the Palácio da Inquisição. The baroque Casa da Ópera, inaugurated by José I only six months before the earthquake, was the envy of Europe; and on the eve of the disaster the castrato Caffarelli, then at the height of his fame, offered bel canto to a full house.*

The destruction of these monuments to Crown, Church, commerce, and culture deprived Lisbon of the cardinal points that sustained a sentiment of national identity, but as potent as these symbols were, they bespoke only part of the tragedy. Over the centuries innumerable less grandiose entities and institutions had together created a delicate urban fabric. Burned and buried too were once-bustling markets and taverns, as well as shops and trading companies that sold the exotic goods—pepper, tobacco, cacao,

---

*In thanksgiving for having survived the earthquake, Caffarelli immediately retired from the opera stage and thereafter sang exclusively in churches.

precious woods, and silks—that had made Portugal rich; artisan
workshops like those of the goldsmiths, where bullion was transformed into gilded finery; popular theaters that offered the un-
schooled masses performance in the vernacular; and a host of other
civic associations, religious fraternities, guilds, and charitable organ-
izations. Lisbon was composed of scores of barrios—the Moorish
Alfama, the elegant Barrio Alto, and the Graça, Mouraria, and Alcântara among them—but their destruction would not have affected
Lisbon in the same manner. The Baixa was the heart and soul of
the capital, and Lisbon was inconceivable without it, like London
without the City, or Rome without the Palatine. And yet the Baixa
was gone. Shaken to its foundation, burned to its core, and stripped
of all its life, Lisbon's historic center was an urban wasteland.

On December 4, little more than a month after the quake, the
earth continued to seize with aftershocks. Many streets remained
full of debris, bodies were still being disinterred from the rubble,
and foreign aid was yet to arrive. On this day Manuel da Maia,
chief engineer to the realm, presented his plans for the rebuilding
of Lisbon. Others may have dismissed or discouraged the restoration of Lisbon as pure folly, but engineer Maia, age seventy-eight,
was undaunted. In truth, he was something of an anomaly for
Portugal, a man of exceedingly humble origins (his father had
been a stone-cutter) and little formal education who had risen to
one of the highest appointed positions in the kingdom. For want
of means and social connections, Maia had joined the army as a
young man and begun a slow but determined rise in the ranks.
What he lacked in schooling, he made up for by reading vora-
ciously, especially military history and the art and science of
fortification, yet he never abandoned peasant common sense.
Maia's life was a chronicle of competence and proof that, even in
a country where noble blood and personal connections were

seemingly all important, merit too was rewarded. He fought against the Spaniards at Badajoz, modernized fortifications along the frontier, completed a highly scientific survey of Lisbon, built the monumental Aqueduto das Águas Livres with Custódio Vieira and Carlos Mardel, organized the royal archives, and otherwise looked after a bevy of royal palaces and possessions. He was a member of the Academia Real da História and chronicler of the House of Bragança. Had Maia benefited from social advantages and a proper education, there's no telling what else he might have achieved.

Manuel da Maia's proposal, or *Dissertação* as he called it, for the reconstruction of the capital was addressed ostensibly, like most official documents, to the king, but it was actually presented to Carvalho, who monopolized all decisions regarding the fate of Lisbon. Like all of Maia's work, the proposal was thorough, amply detailed, and practical; it consisted of five distinct options for the capital, ranging from outright abandonment to the construction of a new city atop the ruins of the old, as well as a summary of the advantages and disadvantages of each scheme. If Carvalho had had any doubts about entrusting the rebuilding of Lisbon to a military engineer rather than to an architect, they were likely soon dispelled. Manuel da Maia's knowledge of Lisbon was clearly encyclopedic on account of his years living in the capital, his work on the aqueduct, and, most important, his survey of the city in 1718. Moreover, placing a military man at the helm of the reconstruction would impose a certain regimented discipline to the works, which promised to be as drawn out and troublesome as any protracted military campaign.

The first of Maia's options called for rebuilding Lisbon much as it was before the disaster, using the materials from the ruins. This would be the cheapest and most expedient solution, and the absence of any significant alterations in the urban landscape would avoid legal entanglements with affected property owners. It would also, however, constitute a complete repudiation of urban planning and a missed opportunity of historic proportions for Lisbon. A similar respect for property rights had caused London to let slip a brilliant urban scheme by Christopher Wren in the aftermath of the Great London Fire of 1666, a case with which both Maia and Carvalho were undoubtedly familiar. And restoring Lisbon to its prequake condition would mean recapitulating age-old shortcomings like excessively narrow and irregular streets and high buildings, which had exacerbated the damage and recovery efforts of the earthquake and fire. Such a scenario, warned Maia, "supposed that the earthquake of the past is not a prognosis of another."[2]

The second and third of Maia's options respected the essential plan of old Lisbon but proposed widening certain principal streets and imposing height restrictions on buildings. In the fourth option Maia boldly suggested razing the entire Baixa quarter, or what remained of it, using the rubble to create an expansive foundation, and "laying out new streets without restraint." A modern city would grow up atop the foundation of the old, and the new urban landscape would be governed by strict codes and edifying proportions in which "the width and the height of the buildings should never exceed the width of the streets." The plan would allow for modern sanitary installations, like a sewage system, proper drainage, and generous space for pedestrians and carriage traffic—in short, an enlightened use of space in keeping with the latest notions of urban planning.

Maia's last option, and the one he personally favored, called for building an entirely new capital between Alcântara and Pedrouços, in the vicinity of Belém, and "disdaining ruined Lisbon." It was clearly Maia's most radical proposal but was hardly far-fetched; the area around Belém had suffered only minor damage from the quake, and it was close enough to old Lisbon (approximately four miles) to make the transition less traumatic than, say, moving the capital to Coimbra or Porto.* Maia was understandably wary of building anew in Lisbon; the loss of several quays on the waterfront near the Terreiro do Paço, which had been literally swallowed up by the river, made him especially uneasy. "The sinking of the new Tobacco Customs House Quay seems to be a warning not to get close to a place that shows that it is weakened and can be shaken again, plus everything around it."

Carvalho, it seems, felt otherwise. The first four options were all debatable, but the fifth was inconceivable. After all, Carvalho hadn't risked his life and battled to save Lisbon only to see the capital abandoned. The fear of future calamities, he thought, was exaggerated and contributed to a sense of fatality that was rendering the city feeble. Lisbon had not been plagued by periodic devastating earthquakes as had, for example, Naples, although an earlier earthquake in the sixteenth century had done considerable damage. Despite the severity of the All Saints' disaster, the city could well go another millennium or more without another quake. For an engineer like Manuel da Maia, the idea of transposing the capital might have made perfect sense, but for Carvalho, vital economic, political, and social issues were at stake that he could ill afford to ignore. It wasn't merely Lisbon that he was concerned about but the fate of the monarchy and Portugal's economic viability as a nation as well. Quitting Lisbon would be attributed to the king and universally interpreted as a sign of capitulation. The aura of the capital could not be simply shifted to a new site, nor could the

---

*The area west of Lisbon, including Belém, sits on a foundation of volcanic rock known as the Lisbon Basalt Complex that proved more resistant to seismic activity than Lisbon proper.

affairs of city and state be virtually suspended while the herculean task of building a new capital dragged on for years; it would be an invitation to chaos, the one state that no worthy king could allow and few monarchies could survive. The commercial implications were worse still. Unless the king made a determined, unambiguous stand on Lisbon's recovery, merchants would soon take their business elsewhere, and Portugal, a country of scattered, unscientific agriculture and scant industrial base, would sink into the kind of economic ruin that no quantity of Brazilian gold could ameliorate.

The disaster nonetheless also offered a singular opportunity for renewal. The Enlightenment's new spirit of urban planning was gaining ground throughout Europe, bringing with it the promise of social progress. Order, regularity, proportion, symmetry, and light could be imposed on a physical landscape, and as a consequence man, a creature of his surroundings and environment, would experience a regenerative transformation and come to be governed by reason. Or so went the sunny logic. Architecture was placed in the service of a utopian vision. Here, Carvalho could see at once, was the opportunity to effect the kind of social and economic change that was necessary to rouse Lisbon, and Portugal, from centuries-old slumber. He rejected Maia's options that called for essentially rebuilding Lisbon to its medieval cast; what Lisbon needed, he insisted, was the kind of bold reform embodied in Maia's fourth option. The Baixa would be razed, and a new center would emerge that would serve as a model, a beacon for the rest of the city and the outside world, signaling that a new Lisbon had risen from the ashes like a phoenix. Carvalho chose this shining vision of a revivified capital, and King José I, not one to deny his minister, wisely consented.

At seventy-eight, Manuel da Maia was in the twilight of a long and eminent career in the service of three monarchs. He was well aware that he could initiate the rebuilding of Lisbon but was unlikely to see the project completed. He saw his role as that of an experienced, impelling mentor, and he gathered around himself a group of talented collaborators who would have the vigor and the capability to realize the monumental project. They were a decidedly martial lot, including Lieutenant Colonel Carlos Mardel, the Hungarian-born architect-engineer and member of the circle of Estrangeirados; Captain Eugénio dos Santos, chief architect for the City Senate; Captain Elias Sebastião Poppe; and Lieutenant Gualter da Fonseca.

They were all military engineers by training, but Mardel and Santos were also first-rate architects with experience in civil projects. Mardel had collaborated with Maia on the aqueduct; he had built the Palácio da Águias and the Palácio de Lázara Leitão, both of which introduced elements of the central European baroque to Lisbon; and under João V he had been the architect in charge of royal palaces and military orders. Mardel was brilliant, urbane, and—of no little consequence—a close personal friend of Carvalho. Eugénio dos Santos, age forty-five, was an energetic subordinate of Maia's and, as Lisbon's principal municipal architect, had overseen works all over the capital.

Maia gave each of these architects extraordinary liberty to create plans for the remodeling of the Baixa. He established the parameters of the terrain between the Terreiro do Paço and Rossio squares, which would constitute the nucleus of the works, and he insisted that all the land occupied by churches be respected, that modern sanitary installations be considered, and that a sense of symmetry reign. But otherwise he confined his directives to purely technical matters. The architects were free to propose, and Maia and Carvalho to dispose.

Maia urged Mardel, Santos, Poppe, and Fonseca to examine two foreign projects in particular that might serve as inspirations for their own designs: Christopher Wren's audacious albeit unrealized scheme for London in the wake of the Great Fire, and Filippo Juvarra's early eighteenth-century expansion of Turin for Vittorio Amedeo II, Duke of Savoy and King of Sicily. Both Wren and Juvarra had looked to antiquity for inspiration in imposing an orderly framework of streets and squares on an urban landscape, but the circumstances of topography in London and Turin were wholly distinct from those of Lisbon. Juvarra had the luxury of planning a new town alongside old Turin in virtually virgin terrain; he was thus able to project his new vision of broad public squares and wide, straight boulevards without demolishing existing buildings or clashing with interests of property owners. Consequently the Turin project was, according to Maia, "more a diversion than work," as he wrote in his *Dissertação*, but as a model of matchless scale and proportion, Juvarra's plan was close to flawless.

Wren's scheme for rebuilding London along classical lines, with uniform tree-lined avenues radiating from a central square, especially captivated Maia, although he could get his hands on only one of the Englishman's plans, and it lacked sufficient detail. Wren's project for London was not only an example of enlightened urban design but also a cautionary tale of the power of property owners to stifle change in the urban fabric. King Charles II had initially approved Wren's design, but the noble families who were the principal landowners in central London protested so fiercely that the king withdrew his support. Wren had the not-small consolation of rebuilding more than fifty of London's churches, including St. Paul's Cathedral, but the city lost out on an urban plan that would have made it the paradigm of an enlightened metropolis.

The Lisbon architects could draw upon numerous other examples of modern city planning, such as John Wood the Elder's

Palladian-style schemes in Bath, England; the faubourgs of Paris; and the new quarters in German towns such as Erlangen and Neuwied, to name a few. But the most immediate models for towns laid out systematically came, curiously enough, from the Spanish and Portuguese colonial settlements in Latin America, where strict grids of perpendicular streets and squares were the norm.

Throughout the winter and early spring of 1756, while the architects were hunched over their drafting tables rendering schemes for the future Baixa, the scene on the ground remained desperate. A full-fledged shantytown had sprung up in the center of the city, precisely where Carvalho, Maia, and their team of architect-engineers were envisioning a Lisbon reborn. Rumors of the Baixa's transformation had led anxious former residents to stake their claims by building makeshift huts and shelters atop the ruins that were once their homes. An edict issued in December 1755 forbade any building, temporary or otherwise, in the areas destroyed by the earthquake, but it had been largely ignored; many survivors simply had nowhere else to go and lacked the means to build a shelter on the outskirts of town. The government was sympathetic but intractable. On January 31 three hundred soldiers were deployed in central Lisbon to clear the zone of squatters. They met with little resistance (who, indeed, would have had the will to fight after the ordeal of the quake?) but aroused much resentment. A week later a new edict ordered all illegal constructions destroyed, creating, as it were, ruins atop the ruins.

Carvalho was behind the strong-arm tactics, and his measures, however necessary, were creating a legion of critics and outright enemies. The clergy were now mocking the recovery effort. A growing number of refugees were disgruntled: nobles, who were jealous of Carvalho's authority and sway over the king; and local and foreign merchants, who had been slapped with a special 4 percent tax on all imported goods to help pay for the construction of the new Customs House. Even in far-off Brazil colonists were smarting on account of a munificent *donativo* of three million cruzados for Lisbon's recovery. But as long as Carvalho had the king's blessing—and by every indication it was total—the minister was immune from public criticism and above reprimand. He knew who his enemies were, Jesuits and recalcitrant nobles mostly, and he would deal with them when the circumstances allowed. In the meantime Carvalho focused his considerable energies on Lisbon's resurrection, knowing full well that his fate, not to speak of that of the capital, depended on it.

On April 19 Manuel da Maia presented a final installment of his *Dissertação,* accompanied by six proposed plans for the rebuilding of central Lisbon, to the king and his minister. The detailed plans by Mardel, Santos, Poppe, and Fonseca were above all a tribute to the school of Portuguese military engineering and to Maia's sound guidance. The designs were bold, even visionary, marked by a surprising grasp of the principles of harmony, symmetry, and proportion that were the hallmarks of the emerging urban planning. One plan for the rebuilding of the Baixa, plan number five, by Captain Eugénio dos Santos, enthralled Carvalho and by extension King José I. Superimposed upon the ruins of Lisbon and the still-fresh memories of the old medieval city would be an expansive new Baixa of broad avenues, uniform perpendicular streets, symmetrical blocks of buildings, and monumental squares. If Carvalho had hoped for a rational design that would infuse the capital with a new spirit of order and progress, he had clearly found it. Santos's Baixa was a strict grid laid out on a north-south axis, with the Rossio and the Terreiro do Paço at each pole. The two squares were linked by three broad avenues, or *ruas nobres* (noble streets), which in turn were traversed by seven linear cross streets;

the former were fixed at sixty feet in width, of which fifty feet were reserved for the roadway and ten for the sidewalk, and the latter would be forty feet in width. After the narrow and crooked medieval lanes to which the populace had been accustomed, these new thoroughfares seemed positively cavernous. The plan proposed forty rectangular buildings with a north-south orientation and twelve with an east-west orientation, plus three buildings that were square and one that was oddly trapezoidal. This subtle variation in the buildings' alignment was enough to avoid an excessive sense of monotony and give the whole a certain dynamism. Each block of buildings was four stories tall and contained a central patio that allowed for ample light to reach the interiors. The facades were rigorously consistent in both length and height and bore uniform windows, doors, balconies, eaves, and cornices, which gave the succession of buildings the grand look of one seamless palace. The whole architectural conjunction was at once noble and, at least for the traditionally baroque tastes of the Portuguese, refreshingly understated.

The architectural centerpiece of Santos's design was his treatment of the Terreiro do Paço, in which the architect displayed an astute understanding of the political inclinations and commercial priorities of Carvalho, the project's guiding light and the one man with the power to accept or reject any of the proposed plans. The historic riverside square was the most symbolically charged public space in Lisbon; it had been the site of the Royal Palace, the Casa da India, the Customs House, and many of the principal trading companies, all of which, alas, had been leveled and scorched by the quake and fire. But even before the disaster, the Terreiro do Paço had become something of a muddled space. It had few architecturally distinguished buildings, save the Royal Palace; a fort, the Customs House, and assorted warehouses and quays obscured the view of the Tagus; and the whole terrain—more an expanse than a formal square—lacked spatial and architectural unity.

Santos's scheme would enclose the square on three sides: the Arsenal would occupy the western flank where the palace had stood, the new Customs House would rise on the eastern edge, and the Civil Tribunals would line the square to the north. The south side of the Terreiro do Paço would be open to the Tagus, with nothing to impede the river view. The architectural idiom for all of the buildings was of a piece: rigorously neoclassical. A vaulted arcade of seventy-eight uniform arches, running beneath the buildings, lined the square, providing for a sense of visual and spatial continuity. Of the three *ruas nobres* that led into the square from the north, the central street would be spanned by a triumphal arch. At the center of the square, a colossal pedestal would bear an equestrian statue of King José I. Santos, needless to say, clearly knew who his patrons were. His design for the Terreiro do Paço was an unabashed tribute to King and Commerce, precisely the two pillars on which Carvalho hoped to build the powerful state that would usher in a modern and prosperous Portugal. The minister promptly gave Captain Eugénio dos Santos the nod; the Baixa project, the single most ambitious building scheme in the history of Portugal, was his.

In June Eugénio dos Santos was appointed director of the newly established Casa do Risco, or Drafting House, which would oversee all plans for the reconstruction; Mardel, Poppe, Fonseca, and scores of other mostly military engineers joined him. Construction, however, did not commence for another two years due to legal wrangles with property owners, opposition from the Church (which was still preaching repentance), and a general paucity of funds. At last, in the spring of 1758, construction was inaugurated by royal decree: "The King makes it known by this decree, which bears the force of law, that the city of Lisbon will be promptly rebuilt in accordance with a regular and decorous plan, and the advantages that a new capital will bestow upon Kingdom and State . . . And in order to carry out a work so useful and necessary for the Common Good, neither should there be delays, which would be intolerable, nor should any subject suffer losses."[3] The decree went on to stipulate that property owners would receive the right to build in proportion to the size of their former dwellings, that all construction had to conform to the official plans, and that residents had five years in which to rebuild. The king also offered advantageous mortgages backed by the Crown.

Again, the decree was Carvalho's through and through, and inspired widespread if not universal discontent. Refugees from the Baixa had been living for more than two years in precarious make-shift shelters, forbidden to rebuild their former homes as they saw fit; they were understandably fed up. Some balked at the five-year limit imposed on construction. But the most inflamed opposition came from conservative nobles who regarded Santos's spare, re-petitive designs for their future homes as not only aesthetically distasteful but socially dangerous, since architectural uniformity implied a kind of subversive egalitarianism. After all, there would be nothing to distinguish a noble's house from that of a merchant or, worse, a grocer. The government squelched the critics by of-fering to buy out anyone unwilling to go along with a project designed for the common good; more than a few took the offer, pocketed the three hundred thousand *reis* (the standard compen-sation), and moved to the outskirts of town, where they could build at will and in a manner more fitting to their social station.

All the while, at the Casa do Risco, Santos's grand plan was being imbued with all the necessary details before construction got under way. Here many of the Baixa's most innovative archi-tectural and structural details were hashed out. From the start money was scarce, so the vast building scheme had to be economically viable. The sobriety of Santos's design for the blocks of Baixa houses was due as much to the need to keep construction costs to a minimum as to any aesthetic preference. Precisely the regularity of Santos's facades, and the repetition of doors, windows, balconies, socles, cornices, and other architectural elements, enabled the engineer to devise a series of standardized prefabricated building components for the project. Stone-cutters and carpenters could work off site and bring the prefab elements of, say, window frames to the construction ground when needed. It was not the birth of prefabrication—the technique had sometimes been used in timber-frame construction in northern Europe—but it was the first time that such a modern, standardized building mode would be employed on so grand a scale.

The engineers also had to consider dreaded future disasters. Manuel da Maia had always expressed a reluctance to rebuild Lisbon on its traditional site for fear of another seismic calamity; now he urged Santos to think of structural measures that might mitigate a future earthquake. The engineer came up with two ingenious techniques that gave his buildings a quake-resistant elasticity. The first addressed seismic instability at the buildings' foundations: Santos's houses would go up not on traditional stone foundations but on mammoth wooden piles driven into the ground and in turn topped by a grid of pine trunks, which allowed the edifices to essentially float above the precarious terrain. Second, Santos devised an intricate wooden frame, which he dubbed the *gaiola*, or cage, that would be embedded in the houses' masonry walls. The strength of the *gaiola* was based on the structural resistance of the triangle; the frame was composed of rectangular wooden modules divided into eight roughly equal triangles (imagine the Union Jack), which together proved at once elastic and capable of bearing extraordinary stress. Just to confirm Santos's theory, Colonel Carlos Mardel had a model *gaiola* built in the Terreiro do Paço and ordered troops to march over it, crash into it, and otherwise whack, maul, and drub it, but they were unable to bring it down.

These seismic-resistant construction techniques were the first to be systematically applied in Europe (in this area the Japanese had centuries of experience and were far ahead of the Continent), and they are a tribute to the ingenuity of a modest military engineer whom history scarcely mentions. Alas, the Baixa may have killed him. Eugénio dos Santos died at the age of forty-nine in August 1760, only months after the building of his visionary urban plan got under way. Captain Carlos Mardel was appointed Santos's successor at the head of the Casa do Risco, and he, Maia, and Carvalho made sure that Eugénio dos Santos's plan did not die with him. Construction proceeded ever so slowly, but no significant part of Santos's design for the Baixa was ever abandoned or modified. It was, however, duly emulated. Over time the Baixa plan became a well-known model for enlightened town planning, and a century later both Baron Haussmann and Ildefonso Cerdá, to name but two, drew from Santos in their ambitious transformations of Paris and Barcelona, respectively.

All of Eugénio dos Santos's efforts, and those of Manuel da Maia and of a whole corps of engineers, builders, craftsmen, and laborers would have been in vain had not Minister Carvalho displayed the will and wielded the necessary power to bring about Lisbon's renewal. It was a daunting undertaking, and a democratic process it was not. The minister was not one to seek advice on the restoration, except from his engineers on technical matters, nor did he seem to need it. Between the early postquake planning in 1755 and the initiation of construction in 1760, scarcely a month went by in which he did not issue a decree, edict, or directive to push the rebuilding forward. It was Carvalho who had tapped Santos, selected his design, determined the rights and obligations of property owners, set the timetable, and controlled the pace and funds for the restoration. He knew precisely what his new Lisbon would look like and how it would be organized, right down to the names of the streets. In a decree from November 1760 Carvalho assigned names to the Baixa's streets and specified the guilds that would occupy them: Rua dos Sapateiros for the shoemakers, Rua dos Douradores for the goldsmiths, Rua dos Retroseiros for the haberdashers, and so on. The grander streets were graced with names that were sure to flatter the Crown: Rua Augusta, Rua Nova d'El Rei (New King Street), and Rua Bela da Rainha (Beautiful Queen Street). The Terreiro do Paço became the Real Praça do Comércio. In recognition of all his efforts to designate in favor of Commerce and the Crown, history paid fitting tribute to Carvalho, the future Marquês de Pombal, by naming the heart of the city that had been so thoroughly ravaged by the disaster and then was so miraculously reborn, the Baixa Pombalina.

Ironically, just when Carvalho, Maia, and their colleagues were toiling to rebuild, foreign travelers began to arrive in Lisbon, eager to witness firsthand some of the scenes of absolute destruction that they had experienced vicariously through gazettes, the writings of Voltaire, sermons, and a glimpse of rude engravings. It wasn't the new, model Lisbon springing up in the Baixa that these Grand Tour travelers wished to see, but the effects of the threefold debacle of earth, sea, and fire. What they wanted, in a word, was ruins. Lisbon could certainly deliver ruins, but not the sort of ancient ones that had worn slowly over time, inspired panegyrics, and grown into cultural icons of a distant past. Lisbon's wasted landscape was far more immediate and sinister because it lacked the patina of age. Only a few years before, in this ruined place, a magnificent city had stood, and its demise had come on not slowly, with a dip into decadence and a long, lament-filled decline, but rather in a single day. The ruins of the ancients, potent symbols of an imaginary utopia, evoked pangs of longing for a lost golden age. The sight of Lisbon, a living scene of dystopia, produced only horror. "Mercy!" wrote the Italian literary critic Giuseppe Baretti. "It is impossible to describe the horrible view represented by those ruins now and maybe for the next century or more; because it will take at least a century to clean up." Baretti arrived in Lisbon from London in September 1760, leading the young English lord Edward Southwell on a Grand Tour of Portugal, Spain, France, and Italy. The letters that he wrote home to his brothers in Turin were later published as an epistolary travelogue entitled *Lettere familiari di Giuseppe Baretti a' suoi tre fratelli tornando da Londra in Italia nel 1760*, and the book's most striking scenes depict a Lisbon still in shambles nearly five years after the earthquake. To underscore the destructive force of "the most terrible and unopposable of all natural violent events," Baretti described for his brothers the ruins of the Paço da Ribeira, implying that not even the loftiest palace could withstand Nature's fury:

> If only you could see the royal palace, such an astounding sight, my brothers. Try to envision a structure of quite beautiful architecture, all made of marble and huge stones, broad and squat rather than high, with the principal exterior walls more than three feet wide, and which encompassed a perimeter that would have been sufficient to contain not just the court of the king of Portugal but also that of an emperor of the Orient; and yet this structure, which should have been as solid as a mountain of bronze because of its thick walls and moderate height, was so severely damaged by the violent shaking that restoration is not possible.[4]

Baretti's phrase "If only you could see . . ." conveyed the sense that Lisbon's state was ineffable. No description of the ruins, however minutely observed, could possibly do justice to the scope of the catastrophe or the magnitude of the loss. Indeed, "seeing" a city that had been purged of its tangible physical past was a hopeless exercise. In the end, what remained of Lisbon was what remained in the memories of the survivors, and only through their stories of death, loss, turmoil, and survival could the disaster be properly framed, although the people, as Baretti discovered, were ruined too:

> A stranger wandering among those pitiful ruins hears thousands of such moving accounts recited by those accompanying him; and one person interrupts the other to tell him another story more cruel than the first; and whoever passes by and notices other people's interest stops suddenly, and with gestures full of fear and an expression of mourning, and in a still-trembling voice, although five years have passed since that fateful day, recounts the painful story of his misfortunes and the irreparable losses he has suffered, and then leaves with a sigh, filled with sadness.[5]

Foreign visitors like Giuseppe Baretti had come to contemplate ruins and were duly shocked by the devastation, but they underestimated the human forces that were struggling for the city's and their own survival. Lisbon's future was far from secure, mountains of rubble were still piled high, wounds remained fresh, and a sea of refugees was seething. Still, the city had no alternative to the imperative of rebuilding—aside from a further lapse into ruin.

CHAPTER EIGHT

ENLIGHTENMENT AT ANY PRICE

[Carvalho] wanted to civilize the nation and at the same time to enslave it. He wanted to spread the light of philo-sophical science and at the same time elevate the royal power of despotism.

> —António Ribeiro dos Santos, chronicler and
> librarian at the University of Coimbra

On a clear September night in 1758 King José I, accompanied by his royal valet Pedro Texeira, was returning to Belém by coach from the palace of the Marquês and Marquesa de Távora, on the northern outskirts of Lisbon. The king, it appears, had been out consummating his liaison with one of the Távoras' daughters-in-law, and for reasons of discretion he rode in Texeira's carriage. On a little-traveled road in the dead of night, three masked horsemen stopped the coach; a musket shot was fired; and the king was wounded in the arm and shoulder. The horsemen fled, and the coach sped back to Belém with the bleeding monarch. Carvalho was awakened at his hut near the royal camp at Belém and rushed to the king's side. The wound, thankfully, was minor, but the crime—attempted regicide, or so Carvalho chose to see it—was grievous. The incident was kept secret and the king lay low, indisposed, while he recovered. The minister's spies and informers soon identified two of the alleged horsemen, duly arrested them, and mercilessly tortured them. Their confessions, obtained on the rack, implicated none other than the Marquês de Távora. The next morning the two would-be assassins were quietly hung.

Carvalho did not move immediately against Távora; rather, he had the marquês and his family watched, intercepted their mail, and noted their movements scrupulously. Anxious to quell any seditious rumors of a plot against José I, Carvalho attributed the king's temporary absence from the public sphere to a domestic accident in the royal household. Naturally, this bit of ministerial spin was dutifully published in the *Gazeta de Lisboa:* "Our Lord the King, due to a fall suffered in his Palace, was bled on the fourth day of the month as a beneficial remedy . . . May His Majesty get well, which is what all his faithful vassals desire."

By December the minister had uncovered what he believed to be a conspiracy by disaffected nobles to oust José I from the throne and replace him with the Duque de Aveiro. Troops were dispatched to round up the culprits. They were no run-of-the-mill nobles but some of the wealthiest and most distinguished in the kingdom. Francisco de Assis de Távora, age fifty-five, was the third Marquês de Távora and the former viceroy of India; his brother-in-law, José de Mascarenhas, age fifty, was the eighth Duque de Aveiro, the eighth Conde de Santa Cruz, the fifth Marquês de Gouveira, and the hereditary grand marshal of the royal household; in noble rank, he was second only to the king. Arrested along with Távora and Aveiro were their wives and children, a smattering of noble friends, a few loyal servants, the Marquesa de Távora's confessor and Carvalho's old nemesis Father Gabriel Malagrida, and a dozen other Jesuits.

Given the severity of the crime, a special tribunal was formed, and the customary legal procedures and solicitousness afforded nobles were dispensed with; that is to say, coercion and torture were permitted. On the rack the Duque de Aveiro confessed to the conspiracy, and the once-loyal servants turned on their former masters and implicated the entire Távora family in the plot. The Duque de Aveiro; the Conde de Atoguia; and the Marquês and Marquesa de Távora, their two sons, and three servants were sentenced to death. Malagrida and the other Jesuits were thrown in the dank dungeon beneath the Tower of Belém.

The show trial was a mockery; the evidence and confessions obtained under torture were dubious; and the conspiracy theory was just that, a theory. The attempted regicide may have been less a question of state affairs than of the overwrought reaction of Luis Bernardo de Távora, the cuckholded husband. (One couldn't really blame him. What to do when your wife is entangled with another man who happens to be the king?) Indisputably Távora, Aveiro, and scores of other Portuguese nobles looked upon Carvalho and his spirit of reform with suspicion if not outright hostility. The minister, after all, was a relentless champion of an invigorated merchant class and of a powerful state vested in the Crown, both of which diminished the traditional privileges and influence of the noble ranks. The grandees and the reformer were destined to clash, but that the grandees were intent on conspiracy and a palace coup is questionable at best. To Carvalho, it scarcely mattered. The opportunity to strike a blow not just to the nobility but to the grandees, the cream of the aristocratic crop, was irresistible. A pronounced whiff of personal vengeance was at play. As a young man about Lisbon, Carvalho had sought the hand of one of the Távora girls, only to be roundly rebuffed. The son of a petty *fidalgo*, a mere country squire, it was made clear, was an unthinkable match for the daughter of a grandee. Evidently he never forgot the snub.

The execution, painstakingly staged by Carvalho for maximum effect, was as sadistic a spectacle as anything the Inquisition might have orchestrated. On January 13, 1759, the conspirators were led to the central square in Belém, where the entire royal family, most of the city's nobles, a jeering crowd, Carvalho, and an ominous scaffold awaited them. The marquesa was the first to go, but not before being shown the instruments of torture that would be used on the rest of her family. She was then beheaded. The rest fared worse. The Marquês de Távora and his two sons, along with the Duque de Aveiro, the Conde de Atoguia, and two others were tied to X-shaped crosses; executioners then broke their arms and legs with sledgehammers, forced them to watch as they burned a servant alive, and then strangled the lot. All the while the crowd cheered the fall of the mighty. The gruesome scene lasted most of the day, after which the scaffold and the bodies of the victims were burned and the ashes dumped in the Tagus. The Távora and Aveiro families were stricken from the noble registry; at their numerous estates, the family coats of arms were chiseled from the facades and the gardens were strewn with salt to symbolize barrenness.

The significance of the savagery was lost on no one, least of all the nobles, many of whom beat a hasty retreat to their country estates to escape the scrutiny of Carvalho and his spies. But the Távora plot only emboldened the minister, particularly after José I granted him the title of Conde de Oeiras for his efforts. He proceeded to unleash a reign of terror in which thousands of the king's and the minister's alleged enemies were either imprisoned or banished to the colonies. No one was safe. Even the king's illegitimate sons, the "Palhavã Boys," who had offered shelter and succor to many earthquake survivors, were sent into internal exile in Buçaco, a backwater north of Coimbra, where presumably they could do no harm. The king, from either inertia or cowardice, did nothing to curb the excesses of his minister, and Portugal fast descended into full-blown despotism.

With the once-mighty nobles laid low, Carvalho turned his attention to another collective that stood in the way of reform, one far more cunning than the grandees: the Jesuits.

Carvalho knew the Jesuits only too well. They had been his teachers at Coimbra; they were ubiquitous at court, where they exerted a disproportionate influence on the royal family; and they were shrewd players in the commercial activities of their exten-sive missions throughout Latin America and the Indies. If the minister was to institute reforms in education, commerce, and the state's administrative workings, he could not afford to have the Jesuits undermining his every move. Already in 1757 Car-valho had managed to dismiss the three royal confessors, all Jesu-its, and have them replaced with secular priests. When this move drew the ire of the papal nuncio, Carvalho hinted at severing all ties with Rome and establishing a national church of a vaguely Protestant stamp. The Vatican, desperate not to lose one of Cath-olic Europe's most stalwart defenders of the faith and, to boot, a munificent donor to the papal coffers, relented.

Carvalho then took the opportunity to complain to Pope Ben-edict XIV about the illegal trading practices that the Society of Jesus routinely conducted in its colonial missions.* This was a seri-ous charge, and although the pope was undoubtedly aware of the custom, he was obliged to investigate. He appointed Cardinal Saldanha, the patriarch of Lisbon and, as it happened, a close friend of Carvalho's, to pursue the matter. It was, by any measure, an open-and-shut case. San Ignacio, the Jesuits' founder, had strictly forbidden members of the order to accumulate wealth, but the rule had been flagrantly ignored, and by the eighteenth century the Jesuits had become, in addition to educators, royal confessors,

---

*Benedict XIV was no friend of the Society of Jesus; in a breve issued in 1741 he denounced the Jesuits as "disobedient, contumacious, captious and reprobate persons."

and missionaries, members of a vast international trading firm with houses, missions, colleges, churches, plantations, warehouses, and estates scattered around the globe—in a word, a multinational. Cardinal Saldanha's investigation produced a scathing decree against the society, and all of its merchandise was confiscated.

Just when Carvalho must have thought that he had found a pope with whom he could deal, Benedict XIV died in the spring of 1758 and was succeeded by Clement XIII, a staunch defender of the Jesuits. Carvalho would have to find another means to bring down the Society of Jesus. He found it in the conspiratorial miasma of the Távora plot. Building on Gabriel Malagrida's role as the Marquesa de Távora's confessor, Carvalho managed to orchestrate an indictment of the whole order. The Jesuits implicated in the plot had been spared the scaffold at Belém only because they were exempt from the civil courts, but in Carvalho's Portugal there was no impunity or, it would seem, half measures. On September 3, 1759, exactly a year after the attempt on the king's life, Carvalho issued a decree expelling the Society of Jesus from Portugal and all its dependencies; their schools and the University of Évora were closed, and the state confiscated all their property. The Jesuits were rounded up and forced to embark on ships in miserable condition bound for the Papal States.

It was Carvalho's greatest victory; he had crushed one of the most powerful and well-organized forces in Catholic Europe, one that had come to meddle far too much in the internal and external affairs of Portugal. He had eradicated the two-hundred-year legacy of the Jesuits in the kingdom and its colonies in his favorite manner, by decree: "For just reasons known to us, and which concern especially the service of God and the public welfare, we suspend from the power of confessing and preaching, in the whole extent of our patriarchate, the fathers of the Society of Jesus, from this moment, and until further notice."*

In truth, all the Jesuits had been expelled but one. Father Gabriel Malagrida continued to languish in the dungeon beneath the Tower of Belém. Carvalho could have deported him along with the dozen other once-imprisoned Jesuits, but the minister, as was by now abundantly clear, was one to hold a grudge. Few had derided Carvalho's efforts to save Lisbon, rebuild the capital, and diminish the influence of nobles and Jesuits quite so vehemently and with such relish as Malagrida. The ex-missionary was a dangerous enemy; in both Portugal and Brazil he retained the aura of a living saint, a mystic, and an infallible spiritual and earthly guide. His incendiary pamphlet, *An Opinion on the True Cause of the Earthquake,* was still circulating widely and was heeded by thousands of devoted followers. And he had powerful friends who could thwart the minister. Just prior to his arrest, in the midst of Carvalho's persecution of the Jesuits and shortly after the new pope's investiture, Malagrida sent a desperate appeal to Clement XIII that left little doubt of his deep-seated enmity for the minister:

> What a fatal scene. What a grievous spectacle! What a sudden metamorphosis! The heralds of the word of God expelled from the Missions, prescribed and condemned to ignominy . . . and who does this?

---

*In 1767 both France and Spain followed suit, expelling the order from their kingdoms; Naples and Parma soon joined them. Clement XIII, it is said, died in early 1769 of apoplexy brought on by the shock. His successor Clement XIV was eventually forced to dissolve the Society of Jesus in 1773 with his famous breve *Dominus ac Redemptor.*

Not his most Faithful Majesty . . . but the minister
Carvalho, whose will is supreme at court. He, yes, he
has been the architect of so many disasters and seeks to
darken the splendour of our Society, which dazzles his
livid eyes, with a flood of bigoted writings that breathe
an immense, virulent, implacable hatred. If he could
behead all the Jesuits at one blow, with what pleasure
would he do so?[1]

But Carvalho could not behead Malagrida, at least not through
a civil court, so he left him to wither in the dungeon until he died
or his mind gave way. Appeals for his release went unanswered.
When he was not lying prostrate in his cell, praying hard for mar-
tyrdom, Malagrida feverishly transcribed the words of the angelic
voices that he insisted rang in his head. From this otherworldly
collaboration he produced two books of self-proclaimed revela-
tion, which were confiscated by his jailers. The first was a diatribe
on the Antichrist; from a theological perspective, it was more or
less inoffensive. The second work, however, entitled, *The Heroic
and Wonderful Life of the Glorious Saint Anne, Mother of the Virgin
Mary, Dictated by This Saint, Assisted by and with the Approbation
and Help of This Most August Sovereign, and Her Most Holy Son*,
was another matter. It was a delirious tract in which the author
displayed, among other anomalies, an unhealthy fixation on Saint
Anne's uterus. Malagrida had plainly gone mad.

Carvalho hauled the decrepit priest, by now seventy-two, before the Inquisition, to which he had conveniently appointed his
brother, Paulo de Carvalho e Mendonça, inquisitor general. The
tribunal found Malagrida guilty of obscenity and blasphemy and
condemned him to death. The irony was uncanny. Here was the
Holy Office of the Inquisition and the Society of Jesus, the two

most militant institutions produced by the Counter-Reformation, the one devouring the other in the name of orthodoxy. And despite Malagrida's long-established enthusiasm for the Inquisition, his own sentence was no less cruel than that of other victims. Malagrida, as anyone could see, was demented and a threat to no one, but Carvalho would have his way. On September 21, 1761, Malagrida was brought before the throng in the still-ruinous Rossio square and strangled on the garrotte. His corpse was then confined to the flames of a bonfire and his ashes cast into the river.

If European opinion needed any more evidence, after the hair-raising Távora executions, that Portugal was consumed in a terror, Malagrida's murder—and it would be specious to call it anything else—provided it. The barbarity, as always, was attributed to the backwardness of the Portuguese and the Black Legend that enveloped Iberia in a shroud, but the latest violence—nobles submitted to base public executions, and the persecution and expulsion of the Jesuits—was altogether unprecedented, even revolutionary (and provided a taste of the terror to come during the French Revolution). Jesuits and nobles outside Portugal may well have cursed Carvalho and prayed and predicted that he wouldn't last long, but they underestimated the minister's growing appeal to large segments of Portuguese society that had been hitherto disenfranchised. He was the advocate of merchants and traders, New Christians and new thinkers, military men and landless peasants; yet he was no populist, but rather an exponent of a popular monarchy and a liberal economic, social, and legal order capable of stripping away the obstructions to modernity and progress.

By any definition, Carvalho was a despot, but he was indisputably an enlightened one and not so very different from other authoritarian rulers, such as Frederick the Great in Prussia and Joseph II in Austria, who were likewise bent on instituting sweeping reform from above. For all of Carvalho's well-documented cruelty, he did not arbitrarily seek power for its own sake. He did not govern for personal financial gain (contrary to accusations by his enemies), and he resisted promoting a cult to his own person, preferring instead to attribute his achievements to the king. For Carvalho, power was merely a means to impose lasting reform on a society that had grown enervated through submission to an archaic Church and its unbending beliefs, and a firmly entrenched nobility for which change of any nature—political, social, or economic—was resisted on principle. Carvalho's political convictions were neither suddenly nor hastily acquired; on the contrary, his belief in a robust state grounded in an absolute monarchy was a long time evolving. During his diplomatic stints in London from 1738 to 1745 and Vienna from 1745 to 1749, Carvalho had witnessed firsthand, and duly noted, the benefits of enlightened absolutism. From Sir Robert Walpole, British prime minister under George II, he learned the importance of power as a guarantor of independent action, the need to promote a dynamic trading and commercial class, and the supreme role of finance in the survival of a modern state. From Maria Theresa and her chancellor Wenzel Anton von Kaunitz, Carvalho learned about modern administrative reforms, the blessings of centralization, and the necessity of extricating the Church from the affairs of government.

Carvalho was well aware, however, that the task of reform in Portugal would be troublesome because the country was so arrested on nearly every front. The centuries-old problems of obsolete communications, insufficient industry, trade imbalances, social stagnation, and an antiquated education system, all eclipsed by the bright luster of bullion, were preventing Portugal from taking its rightful place among the civilized nations of Europe. The time had come for a comprehensive scheme of reform, and Carvalho was arguably the only man in the realm who could see it through.

From the moment when Carvalho consolidated authority and dominance over King José in the wake of the earthquake, until the monarch's death in 1777, the minister left scarcely a facet of Portuguese life untouched. In the first years after the disaster Carvalho was almost wholly consumed by the plans for Lisbon's reconstruction, but once he had sufficiently tamed the nobility with the spectacle of the Távora plot, and forcibly removed the Jesuits from the scene, the way to more pervasive social and economic reform was all but clear. The expulsion of the Society of Jesus had been accompanied by the opportune confiscation of their considerable property in both Portugal and the colonies, including land, schools, and convents, much of which was promptly sold off to fund the reform campaign.* Few of Carvalho's envisioned reforms would prosper, however, if Portugal's educational system was not modernized and extended to the masses. Illiteracy had always been shockingly widespread, and the country was habitually obliged to import clerks, accountants, and managers from abroad to do the work that should have been in native hands. A school of commerce, the Aula do Comércio, opened in 1759, and two years later one of the Jesuits' former colleges in Lisbon was appropriated as a school for the sons of the nobility (of the pliant sort). Perhaps the minister's boldest educational initiative, however, was the proposed establishment of more than eight hundred national primary and secondary schools (a proposal, sadly, only partially realized), which brought proper education to the multitudes for the first time in Portugal's history.

---

*The Jesuits' accumulated wealth was nearly incalculable. In Brazil alone, as the historian David Birmingham observes in A Concise History of Portugal, "the Jesuits owned some of the richest plantations and most expensive urban real estate in South America. One of their Rio de Janeiro estates covered 100,000 acres and employed 1,000 slaves. They also owned seventeen sugar factories in the lowland plantation zones."

The Inquisition, which for centuries had controlled the populace's intellectual fare by prohibiting any enlightened ideas, or those who spouted them, from gaining a foothold in Portugal, was stripped of its role as censor, and for the first time books on science, philosophy, and history, many of them produced by the newly formed royal printing press, circulated freely. One of the most popular books to emerge in this more tolerant intellectual climate was *Cartas sobre a educação da mocidade* (Letters on the Education of Young People), published in 1760 by the New Christian physician and educator António Ribeiro Sanches. The book, along with Luís António Verney's *True Method of Study*, did much to disseminate empiricism and the blessings of the scientific method: "the true purpose of a young person's education is not that they should be perfect in a particular science, but rather to expose them to understanding, and provide them with the necessary tools to learn whatever it is to which they wish to apply themselves."[2] This kind of pedagogical liberty would have been inconceivable in the old Jesuit-dominated educational system, which prized obedience over curiosity, and doctrine over reason. "Thank God I have lived long enough to receive the news that the priests of the Company of Jesus are no longer Confessors or Masters," wrote Sanches, "for if they had been allowed to continue in such offices, which they had held for so long, all the truths which can be read in these pages would be regarded as nothing more than heresy!"[3]

Censorship, alas, hardly disappeared; it was simply assumed by the new Real Mesa Censória, another of Carvalho's artifices, which banned all works by the Jesuits or anything that could be construed as even vaguely antimonarchical. Oddly enough, it wasn't until 1772 that the censors finally got around to officially purging Gabriel Malagrida's *An Opinion on the True Cause of the Earthquake*. The chief censor, António de Santa Marta Lobo da Cunha, pronounced the book "malicious, temerarious, and heretical," although he added that such a work "could never make a significant impression on men who are truly wise, pious, and free of illusion and fanatical preoccupations." Still, just for good measure, he banned the book and ordered existing copies to be burned, which suggests that Malagrida, or rather his incendiary opinions, were still perceived as a threat to the state more than a decade after his execution.

At the University of Coimbra, which Carvalho had previously described as "a university where stubbornness, sophism and bad books cut a great figure,"[4] the statutes were revised to do away with the overly scholastic model. Mathematics and natural sciences became part of the academic program, and the philosophical works of Montesquieu, Voltaire, the Encyclopedists, Kant, and Locke, among others, were added to the syllabus. In keeping with the new spirit of inquiry, an exquisite botanical garden was laid out and an astronomical observatory built. Carvalho himself became a visiting lecturer. The university was to be considered not an isolated scholastic institution but rather a pedagogical extension of the state, and as such it would be responsive to the state's needs.

And what Portugal needed was *novos homens*, new men who were free of inveterate prejudices and religious fanaticism and attuned to the new notions of scientific, intellectual, and social progress that were the hallmarks of the age. These new men would serve the state in the creation of a newly invigorated Portugal. Francisco de Lemos, the rector of Coimbra University and a close collaborator of Carvalho's, spelled out the symbiosis between state and university that he and the minister hoped would hasten Portugal's transformation into a modern nation:

> One should not look on the university as an isolated body, concerned only with its own affairs, as is ordinarily the case, but as a body at the heart of the state, which through its scholars creates and diffuses the enlightenment of wisdom to all parts of the monarchy, to animate, and revitalize all branches of the public administration, and to promote the happiness of man. The more one analyses this idea . . . the more one sees the mutual dependency of these two bodies one on the other, and that science cannot flourish in the university without at the same time the state flourishing, improving, and perfecting itself. This understanding arrived very late in Portugal, but at last it has arrived.[5]

An educated, enlightened populace, Carvalho reasoned, would surely make his reforms irrevocable. There would be no turning back to the benighted past once subjects had been introduced to the liberating light of reason. This kind of heady, boundless faith in education, reason, and human progress was typical of the age, but in Portugal's case the centuries of ecclesiastically imposed obscurantism made it all the more urgent. *Novos homens* became the catchphrase and title for all those who had been inculcated with a liberal education, civic mores, and a revulsion for superstition.

Carvalho was nothing if not expedient, and many of his most audacious social reforms were undertaken, first and foremost, as means to spur economic prosperity. He is rightly credited, for example, with outlawing slavery in Portugal (if not in the colonies—the Brazilian bonanza would have collapsed without it), but he was motivated less by the lofty humanitarianism of a true abolitionist than by awareness of sheer economic necessity.* Colonial Portuguese who had made fortunes in Brazil were returning to the mother country with their slaves in tow and using them as domestic servants. The flood was depleting the colony of much-needed labor and causing productivity on the plantations and in the mines to plummet, something that Portugal, increasingly dependent on her most prosperous colony, could ill afford. Similarly, Carvalho did away with the odious distinction between Old and New Christians; racial discrimination was outlawed; and all Portuguese subjects, regardless of their descent, became eligible for any state office.

The institutional discrimination against the Jews was a centuries-old problem that had cost the country dearly. Following their expulsion in the late fifteenth century, many of the Jewish families that had preferred exile to conversion went on to prosper as artisans, merchants, and traders—invariably at Portugal's expense—in the Netherlands, England, the Levant, and elsewhere. The New Christians who had converted, often forcibly, and stayed on in Portugal were subject to every manner of persecution, including pogroms, special taxes, exclusion from public office and the university, and persistent social discrimination. For an eighteenth-century European ruler, Carvalho was remarkably free of religious and racial prejudice, especially in light of the furious anti-Protestant and anti-Jewish invectives that had trationally rung from the Portuguese pulpits and had conditioned

---

*The complete abolition of slavery in Brazil did not occur until 1888, long after the colony had acquired independence from Portugal.

generations of "good" Catholics in the art of intolerance. While in London, Carvalho had actively sought out Portuguese Jewish exiles, and the Estrangeirados circle had numerous New Christians. While he seems to have been genuinely concerned with their plight, he was also particularly determined to tap their erudition and commercial acumen for his new Portugal. For Carvalho, social justice and economic exigency were all part of the same grand scheme.

Despite the minister's ulterior motives, both the abolition of slavery and the redress of the Jews marked a profound leveling change in Portuguese society. Henceforth all the subjects in the kingdom—nobleman and commoner, Christian and Jew, former slave and master—were equal before the law. The Inquisition ceased to be a Church-run tribunal and became a civil court. Heretics and Judaizers were no longer burned at the stake. But the flames were far from extinguished; only the victims were changed. Now the condemned were, in the irrevocable semantics of the despot, enemies of the state, and to root them out, a police force was established, whose chief, not surprisingly, was Carvalho.

By the mid-eighteenth century Portugal was sorely dependent on Brazil and Britain for its economic fortunes. The abundance of Brazilian gold and diamonds, the gruesome prosperity of the slave trade, and the successful cultivation of sugar, tobacco, and other agricultural products on the slave-driven plantations of Brazil all combined to sap the Portuguese of entrepreneurial spirit. Portuguese merchants had grown accustomed to simply re-exporting agricultural goods and raw materials to northern Europe for quick, painless profits; and gold paid for the historic and increasingly swollen trade deficit that arose from the imports of grain, wood, textiles, and other essential commodities to Portugal. This absolute dependency of the mother country on its colonial possessions for economic survival, not to speak of prosperity, diminished Portugal's stature among the more formidable European states. Without its colonies, everyone was aware, Portugal would be a third-rate power at best. The Portuguese condition was accurately described by the Chevalier des Courtils, a French traveler who visited Lisbon just prior to the earthquake: "[Portugal] is more of a province than a kingdom. One might say that the King of Portugal is a potentate of the Indies that lodges in a European land. The vast and rich states under his sovereignty in the new world, with Brazil, Rio de Janeiro, Bahia of all the saints, Goa, Madeira, in Africa, the Azores in Europe, have made him a considerable prince and placed him among the number of powerful maritime powers of Europe if one considered the value of his possessions."[6]

All the while Portugal's military alliance with Britain, so vital to protecting the country and its colonies on both land and sea, exacted a high price: a series of disastrous commercial treaties converted Portugal into a quasi–economic colony of Britain. The Methuen Treaty of 1703, which was still in effect after the Lisbon disaster, provided for an easing of duties on British textiles in Portugal in exchange for a similar preference to Portuguese wine exports to Britain; it was a decidedly lopsided arrangement. In *The British Merchant*, a widely read apologia to mercantilism published in London in 1748 by Charles King, the author roundly observed: "By this treaty we gain a greater balance from Portugal, than from any other country whatsoever." The treaty effectively stifled textile and associated industries in Portugal and encouraged the monoculture of the vine. Britain's seemingly insatiable thirst for port drove the Portuguese to focus almost single-mindedly on the wine and cork trades.* In the decade from 1678 to 1687, Portugal exported an average of 632 casks of wine annually; by the mid-eighteenth century, that figure had skyrocketed to nearly twenty thousand casks, the lion's share of which was destined for the British market.[7] Portugal thus neglected alternative crops and the fostering of new industries that would have eased the economic stress during the years when the wine trade suffered from glut, blight, or drought.

British merchants in Portugal, meanwhile, enjoyed virtually the same liberties and privileges as their native counterparts. The laissez-faire attitude of the Portuguese emboldened the British merchants, who increasingly gained the upper hand in the re-export of raw materials from Brazil and elsewhere. The risks of the Brazilian trade were considerable due to the perils of Atlantic crossings, and it often took years for merchants to see a return on their investments in merchandise and credit, but the profit margins, which ranged from 25 to 30 percent on typical transatlantic cargoes, were incentive enough. Droves of British merchants and speculators with an eye to get rich quick flocked to the free-wheeling "London of the south," as they called the Portuguese capital, and to Oporto, often undercutting the traditional British merchants who had been doing business in Portugal for generations. In 1752 Lord Tyrawly, the former British ambassador to Portugal, visited the city and found the British merchant community there much changed; the "traditional, regular, and frugal

---

*Port wine was first developed in the 1670s, when a group of enterprising British merchants found that the traditionally rough wines of the Douro region were much improved by the addition of brandy. A wine so fortified proved more stable during its shipment to Britain, and the British public appreciated its added punch. Port soon became the rage, and port wine cellars sprang up in clubs, universities, and private houses.

merchants" had lost ground to "men of a very different character," he wrote. The new breed of merchants traded "more or at least as Much in French goods, Hamburg linen, Sicilian corn, and other commodities of different countries than in the Produce of their Own."[8] The British presence in Lisbon and Oporto grew so ubiquitous, in fact, that the writer Arthur William Costigan wrote famously, "It is a common observation of the natives, that excepting of the lowest conditions of life, you shall not meet anyone on foot some hours of the violent heat every day, but dogs and Englishmen."[9]

Carvalho was painfully aware of the British dominance in Portuguese trade and commerce. During his diplomatic posting in London he had gained some small advantages for the fledgling community of Portuguese traders in the British capital, but he could not undo the conditions of the Methuen Treaty due to Portugal's military alliance with Britain, nor could he curtail the vast capital with which the powerful British merchants backed their trading ventures and that virtually guaranteed their commercial supremacy. Portugal's only recourse was to embark on a mercantilist policy and industrialization campaign of its own. It would not be the first such effort. A similar initiative was adopted in the late seventeenth century by the Conde de Ericeira, superintendent of factories and manufactures of the realm; it had met with surprising success, and a nascent textile industry had begun to operate in Lisbon, Covilhã, Fundão, and Tomar. The discovery of gold in Brazil, however, soon sank the ventures. In desperation, Ericeira took his own life.

Carvalho had already begun his industrial campaign several years before the earthquake. A national gunpowder factory and a sugar refinery were established in 1751, and a silk industry the following year. But only after his consolidation of power and after

the restoration of Lisbon was well under way did the industrialization effort begin in earnest. A global recession in the 1760s—
which caused Brazilian exports to plummet by 40 percent, gold
revenues to decline, and British imports to Portugal to drop by
half—made the development of home industries all the more urgent. Starting in 1766, state-funded factories manufacturing rope,
glass, ceramics, paper, textiles, hats, and even playing cards
sprouted up throughout Portugal.

At the same time Carvalho attempted to wean the country
from its excessive dependence on British and other foreign traders
by establishing a series of monopolies for both colonial and domestic exports. Charter companies were granted exclusive trading
rights for, among other products, Algarve sardines, Brazilian diamonds, Asian spices, whaling products, and Douro wine. The purpose of these licensed monopolies was to better control economic
activity for the benefit of the state and to simultaneously nurture a
dynamic commercial bourgeoisie to rival the means and influence
of both the Portuguese nobility and the foreign traders. Not everyone benefited from such monopolies, and there were instances of
outright rebellion. In 1757 Oporto erupted in five days of rioting
and pillage, incited by local wine merchants who were being
squeezed out of business by the new monopoly company. Carvalho,
thoroughly in character, interpreted the incident as an attack on
the state and brutally suppressed the uprising; nine of its instiga-
tors were put to death, and seventy-eight conspirators were shipped
off to penal colonies in West Africa. In Carvalho's Portugal nothing was to get in the way of commercial and industrial enterprise
and the supreme authority of the state—and as long as the minister
maintained his firm grip on power, little did.

In 1769 King José elevated Sebastião José de Carvalho e Melo,
Conde de Oeiras, to the peerage of Marquês de Pombal, the title

by which the minister would be remembered by history. His as-
cent from *fidalgo* to grandee had been headlong and unprecedented, and the way strewn with implacable enemies, imperious
decrees, and not a few corpses. On the whole, however, Carvalho
deserved the honor. No Portuguese minister before (or since) had
done more to raise the condition of the kingdom and its subjects.
By the time he was named Marquês de Pombal, Carvalho was
seventy years old; he had only recently escaped an attempt on his
life (the would-be assassin, a Genoese named Giovanni Battista
Pele, was in prison and would eventually be tried, oddly, for attempted "regicide" and summarily drawn and quartered); and he
had outlived many of his most trusted collaborators, including
Manuel da Maia, who had died the year before at the estimable
age of ninety-one; Carlos Mardel, who passed away in 1763; and
the Marquês de Alegrete, president of the Municipal Senate.
Carvalho's most salient reforms were behind him. He had rescued
Lisbon, set the capital's reconstruction scheme in motion, checked
the nobility, liberated the Crown from Church meddling, expelled the Jesuits, abolished slavery, unified the tax code, reformed
the military, fostered commerce, regulated trade, and established
the royal printing press. And those were just the most conspicuous initiatives. In the following years he would concentrate on his
educational reforms, the inauguration of new industries, and the
grooming of his son Paulo for state affairs, but by and large his
legacy was made.

If anything irked the minister in his twilight, it was the sluggish
pace of Lisbon's reconstruction. All the principal engineers who
had been involved in the project from its inception—Maia, Santos,
and Mardel—were gone; a new generation of military engineers
had taken their places, executing what their predecessors had
conceived. The rebuilding was forever hampered by contentious

property owners, a scarcity of building materials and qualified labor, and a paucity of funds, but ever so slowly the new capital took shape. By 1766, little more than a decade after the earthquake, fifty-nine new apartment blocks had gone up in the Baixa, as had hundreds of houses in other barrios scattered across the city. Under normal circumstances such construction would have constituted a veritable building boom, but in a city that had lost a full ten thousand buildings in the disaster, it was a drop in the bucket. Foreign visitors continued to write descriptions of Lisbon's streets piled high with rubble. Shantytowns around Lisbon were still brimming with survivors. Even King José remained in his glorified wooden hut in Belém; in fact, he was so traumatized by the quake that for the rest of his days he refused to sleep under any masonry-sustained roof.

The long-awaited moment to inaugurate the rebuilt Baixa quarter finally arrived in the spring of 1775. In truth, the commencement was slightly premature; twenty years after the earthquake, large parts of the Baixa were still under construction, but the monumental equestrian statue of King José was ready, and Carvalho insisted on using the unveiling ceremony in the new Praça do Comércio as a pretext for an official celebration. The minister was now seventy-six years old and rumored to be suffering from leprosy; the thought of dying before the Baixa was properly finished caused him understandable anguish. The rebuilt city center—with its spacious, light-filled streets, rational architecture, modern sanitary installations, and schematic, regulated commerce—was the physical manifestation of all that Carvalho held dear. The only element missing from the equation had been a sufficiently commanding symbol of the monarchy, and now it was ready.

The unveiling of the equestrian statue and the inauguration of the Baixa took place on June 6, the king's sixty-first birthday. In order to give the unfinished Praça do Comércio a more consummate look, a legion of workers had filled in the gaps between the buildings with mock facades made of wood and plaster. The whole square was festooned with banners and flags and colored lanterns. The royal family took in the spectacle from a discreet second-floor window in the new Customs House, both to avoid the crush of the crowd that packed the square and in deference to Carvalho, the indisputable protagonist of the Baixa's rebirth. Accompanying the minister on the dais were magistrates, representatives of the guilds and commercial associations, merchant princes, the patriarch, some foreign dignitaries, and his son Paulo, who by now was president of the Municipal Senate. There were speeches, and the patriarch said a prayer. The public could barely contain its expectations. And then Carvalho pulled the rope to unveil the monument. The crowd roared, understandably: the towering bronze equestrian statue of King José mounted on an equally towering pedestal was as wondrous a thing as most of the onlookers had ever seen. It was a fitting tribute to a devoted monarch, they said, a monument to inspire awe, a work of unparalleled Portuguese genius.

The sculptor, Joaquim Machado de Castro, had been handpicked for the commission by Carvalho, but the fundamental design of the equestrian statue had been provided by Eugénio dos Santos in his original plan for the Baixa. Santos, for his part, seems to have been wholly inspired by the French sculptors Charles Le Brun and François Girardon, especially the latter, whose bronze equestrian statue of Louis XIV in Paris's Place Louis Le Grand was something of a paradigm of the genre.* Machado's

---

*The statue, alas, was destroyed during the French Revolution, but a diminutive working model of the monument by Girardon can still be seen in the Louvre.

monument, in keeping with the strict neoclassical canons of the day, was ripe with allegorical allusions to ancient grandeur and mythology. The king, looking uncharacteristically commanding on horseback, wears a suit of armor of a vaguely Roman type, a flowing cape, and an extravagantly plumed helmet. In his right hand he bears a scepter, the emblem of royal authority. That José had never donned armor, nor wielded much authority, was, as these genre works went, beside the point. With allegory, anything is possible. The king's horse is in midstep, treading serpents (sin) under hoof. Both king and steed cast their gaze over the vast square and out to the watery expanse of the Tagus. Flanking the base of the pedestal are two sculpture groups in carved stone. On one side, a winged figure of Triumph leads a horse over the trampled figure of an enemy soldier; on the other, a winged figure of Fame leads an elephant over the trampled figure of a slave (an appropriate image for a country that for centuries had traded humans like any other commodity). On the front face of the pedestal is an elaborately carved rendering of the royal coat of arms, directly beneath which is a bronze medallion with a bust of Carvalho in bas relief. The portrait bears little resemblance to the minister, at least compared to the painterly portraits from the same period, but what Machado missed in likeness he made up for in gesture. Carvalho is captured with an unmistakably sardonic smile, as if mocking those who insisted that Lisbon could never be revivified.

The unveiling was followed by three days of unbridled festivities, all deliberately stage-managed by Carvalho for maximum effect. There were processions of floats decorated with allegorical scenes from Portuguese history, fireworks displays, military parades and exercises, an opera performance, poetry readings in Portuguese, French, Italian, Spanish, Latin, Greek, and Hebrew, a ball, a banquet for the commoners (in which four and a half tons of sweets were consumed), and another for the court (in which guests supped from porcelain specially decorated with images of King José's equestrian monument). Lisbon was in exalted spirits for the first time in decades, and no one more so than Carvalho. All that he had gambled, promoted, decreed, and dreamed in the tumultuous years since the earthquake had at last come to fruition in this collective celebration of renewed promise for a city that all but a handful of visionary subjects had thought was tottering (literally) on the brink of the grave. And it was he, Carvalho, the self-made, all-powerful minister, the Conde de Oeiras, the Marquês de Pombal, who had brought it all off. Even the minister's sworn enemies, and they were legion, granted that the transformation of Lisbon had been a prodigious, heroic feat and would not have occurred without so determined and ruthless a figure at the helm. It was Carvalho's finest hour. Who then would have thought that the festivities would mark the minister's last, vainglorious hurrah?

Less than two years after the celebration, King José I, "the Reformer," was dead. When the news reached Carvalho, he rushed to the monarch's deathbed, only to be turned away by Cardinal de Cunha, a former collaborator, who told him laconically: "Your Excellency no longer has anything to do here." The utterance was as shocking as it was inevitable. José's demise spelled Carvalho's political death. For twenty-seven years the king had been the minister's patron and protector, the one man who kept him in power and indulged his every political whim. Now Carvalho was alone, deprived of the royal aura that was the source of both his enterprise and his impunity. Maria Francisca, King José's eldest daughter, assumed the throne as Maria I (she was Portugal's first female sovereign), and she immediately dismissed the minister by royal decree. Both Maria I and the Queen Mother Maria Ana

Victória loathed Carvalho for his progressive ascendancy over King José and his manifest cruelty during the Távora and Malagrida executions. Ironically, the same royal absolutism that Carvalho had so strenuously defended as an engine for change proved to be his undoing. The minister, who had silenced, persecuted, exiled, and condemned in the name of the king, was ultimately a victim of the royal prerogative.

Queen Maria embarked on a reactionary political and social agenda that came to be known as the Viradeira, an obscure Portuguese word that can be roughly translated as "turnabout, upset, or reversion"; and there was little doubt about what she was reverting from, namely, most of the reforms that Carvalho had spent decades tirelessly promoting. She began by releasing more than eight hundred political prisoners whom Carvalho had arbitrarily locked up and beckoning scores of his enemies to return from exile in Spain, France, and elsewhere. The Távora family was posthumously rehabilitated and restored to the peerage. The liberation and return of the ex-minister's adversaries created a vociferous opposition bloc that lost no time in agitating for Carvalho's head. Suddenly the once omnipotent minister seemed to be universally vilified, and his former friends and allies—prosperous merchants, progressive clerics, the new nobles on whom he had bestowed titles, and other enlightened spirits—grew conspicuously silent. He became the stuff of satire. "A Quixotada," a widely read poem by Nicolau Tolentino de Almeida, mocked the fall of the "sad marques" with relish: "Arms engraved in gold/ Which you yourself have raised/And by you drawn/In human blood are bathed/And on a thousand laws are hinged."[10]

More than twenty years had passed since the earthquake, and the memory of the audacity and determination with which Carvalho, the Deliverer, had confronted the disaster had grown faint in the public consciousness. A flood of lawsuits were filed against the ex-minister; his family was persecuted; his house was besieged by hecklers; and in a symbolic beheading, a whipped-up mob tore the bronze medallion bearing Carvalho's effigy from the pedestal of King José's equestrian monument in the Praça do Comércio. Eventually the public outcry grew so shrill that Queen Maria decided that Carvalho was deserving of exemplary justice. He was arrested, submitted to a two-year investigation, and found guilty of abuse of power, fraud, and corruption. Carvalho defended himself against all the charges, but his condemnation and fall from grace were foregone conclusions. In 1781 he was exiled to his country estate in Pombal, south of Coimbra—the queen having judged him too old and infirm to execute—and forbidden to venture within twenty leagues of the court. It was a devastating humiliation, to be sure, but hardly unwarranted and rather more humane than the rough justice that Carvalho had meted out to his enemies.

In the last years of his life Carvalho watched with contempt as many of his reforms were repealed. The influence of the Church and the old nobility was restored; many of the charter companies were abolished; and public officials and administrators who were known to have been sympathetic to the ex-minister's policies were purged. In 1782 Sebastião José de Carvalho e Melo, the Marquês de Pombal, died, as a good many despots have done, in his sleep. He was buried at the Convent of Santo António in Pombal, where the bishop of Coimbra, Francisco de Lemos, a longtime friend, presided at his funeral. The panegyric was delivered by Joachim de Santa Clara, a renowned Benedictine orator.

Carvalho's twenty-seven-year rule over Portugal was fraught with conflicting moral implications. In taking stock of it, no single, unambiguous portrait of the minister emerges, but rather two wholly divergent ones. In his illuminating biography of Carvalho, *Pombal: Paradox of the Enlightenment*, Kenneth Maxwell explains the duality rather starkly: "To some Pombal, who to all intents and purposes ruled Portugal between 1750 and 1777, is a great figure of enlightened absolutism, comparable to Catherine II in Russia, Frederick II in Prussia and Joseph II in the Austrian monarchy; to others he is no more than a half-baked philosopher and a full-blown tyrant." With regard to Carvalho there seems to be precious little middle ground. He was, depending on one's political outlook, social rank, religious persuasion, or economic fortunes, either a deliverer or a dictator, a statesman or an opportunist, a visionary or "a half-baked philosopher." Curiously enough, there is ample evidence to sustain any of these epithets. Undeniably Carvalho's rule over Portugal was a barely disguised tyranny, complete with spies, secret police, censorship, arbitrary arrest without charges, bloated prisons, and a tragically silent populace, which chose to look the other way in the face of government abuses. Anyone could be arrested, tortured, imprisoned, put to death, or exiled, not just Carvalho's outright opponents but timid critics as well. There was nothing benevolent about the minister's despotism; indeed, Carvalho's persecutions to some extent often seemed perversely gratuitous, as if more motives were at play than unyielding statecraft. It has been suggested that King José was behind the pronounced sadism of the Távora executions and that Carvalho was merely fulfilling the royal will; following orders, however, hardly makes for a moral justification, as the history of twentieth-century tyrannies has made all too clear. In any case, he had no such regal alibi for the murder of Gabriel Malagrida. The former missionary may well have been an outspoken enemy of the minister, perhaps even a conspirator, but at the time of his execution Malagrida was ancient, frail, and by all accounts stark raving mad. Carvalho gained nothing from his murder save notoriety, as the historian Paul Hazard has suggested: "One would take it that the Count d'Oyeras [sic] needed the flames of this *auto-da-fé* to proclaim his triumph to Europe."[11]

And yet Carvalho's accomplishments were at least as formidable as his sins were glaring. The abolition of slavery, the elimination of the distinction between Old and New Christians, the eligibility of all Portuguese for state office, and their equality before the law were momentous and urgent changes for a country mired in medieval customs and social mores. His advancement of industry and education was no less remarkable. Carvalho's single-minded ambition was to transform Portugal into a modern state; that he paradoxically "wanted to civilize the nation and at the same time to enslave it," as his contemporary António Ribeiro dos Santos rightly claimed, led to his inevitable downfall. Still, it is hard to imagine what would have befallen Lisbon, and indeed Portugal as a whole, had Carvalho not acted so valiantly and with such steely resolve on All Saints' Day 1755 and during the whole postquake crisis. The disaster seemed to suit him. It was the high-water mark in his public life and the one for which he is deservedly remembered by history. "The word genius is nowadays carelessly used, and has lost much of its power," wrote Marcus Cheke, another of Carvalho's biographers. "But the almost super-human vitality shown by Pombal at the time of the earthquake may justly entitle him to be called a genius in the true sense of the word. His conduct during the crisis impressed itself indelibly on the minds of his countrymen."[12] But not indelibly enough, it would seem, to eclipse his multiple transgressions.

Carvalho's rehabilitation in Portugal was not long in coming—and no wonder. After the minister's death the country was subject to a steady stream of ill fortune that lasted for decades.

Maria I, whose religious fanaticism was extreme even for Portugal, soon went utterly insane, but not before she left the country largely in the hands of clerics.* In 1799 she was succeeded by her son João as regent, who had the impossible task of clinging to absolutism in an age when the French Revolution had ignited the illusions and the fears of the entire Continent. The invasion of Portugal by Napoleonic troops in 1807 prompted the royal family and court to take ignoble flight to Brazil, where they remained comfortably ensconced until 1821. The Portuguese, with the perennial assistance of the British, eventually drove out the French, but the country had been laid waste by the war. It suffered widespread famine, periodic military uprisings, and political turmoil that pitted revolutionary constitutionalists, inspired by the American and French Revolutions, against reactionary absolutists, backed by the Church and the old nobility. And then in 1822 came the blow of all blows: Brazil, the jewel in the Portuguese Crown and the long-exploited land of milk and honey on which Portugal depended for its economic survival, declared independence. By the 1830s Portugal was economically stagnant, isolated, and smoldering in a protracted civil war. Naturally, nostalgia for the firm hand of the Marquês de Pombal grew in direct proportion to the general chaos.

The first sign of Carvalho's posthumous restoration came in 1833, when a royal decree ordered his medallion restored to its proper place on the pedestal of José's equestrian monument in the Plaça do Comércio. But it was King Pedro V (1837–61), a short-lived but enlightened monarch, who undertook Carvalho's formal rehabilitation in 1856 by having the ex-minister's remains

---

*When the British writer William Beckford visited Portugal in 1786, he was told by the queen's son Prince João that "the kingdom belonged to the monks."

brought from the backwater of Pombal to Lisbon, where they were laid to rest with extraordinary pomp in the Church of das Mercês. Finally the transition from rehabilitated minister to full-blown heroic statesman came in 1934, when António de Oliveira Salazar, the head of the Estado Novo dictatorship and no opponent of despotic ways, unveiled the colossal monument to Pombal that rises at the top of Lisbon's Avenida da Liberdade. The bronze statue of Carvalho crowns a rather too lofty pedestal; the minister stands with his left hand resting on the figure of a lion— symbol of power—that stands guard at his side. No ambiguity there. But Carvalho's gaze is most significant; it is cast over the Baixa quarter, the rebuilding of which was arguably his single greatest achievement. The aptly named Baixa Pombalina is a legacy wrought in stone, a consummate tribute of broad, orderly streets, rational architecture, and abundant light. From an aesthetic standpoint, the urban plan has weathered astonishingly well, and it still marks the heart of the capital. Without Carvalho, the Baixa would not exist, nor in all likelihood would Lisbon as a capital. The disaster of All Saints' Day, for all its human and material destruction, made Sebastião José de Carvalho e Melo into the Great Marquês, the Deliverer, and that is how he is remembered today, even if he died beaten and in disgrace.

EPILOGUE

[The earthquake] was more than a cataclysm of nature; it was a moral revolution.

—Joaquim Pedro de Oliveira Martins,
História de Portugal, 1880.

November 1, 2005, All Saints' Day, dawned crisp and cloudless over Lisbon, much as it had 250 years before. There was even a faint northeast breeze. It was a Monday, and many residents had taken advantage of the holiday weekend to escape to the countryside. Lisbon was uncommonly quiet, almost ghostly; and then at precisely nine-thirty in the morning, the instant in which the shocks commenced centuries before, the church bells of Lisbon tolled in unison in remembrance of the tragedy, and the city was awash in a flood of discordant chimes. This annual rite of recollection is also a sign of continuity, a reminder of the horror that brought Lisbon so close to annihilation but also of the city's survival against all odds. For Lisboans, All Saints' is at once a commemoration of cataclysm and renewal.

Celebrating anniversaries is a means of keeping history and collective memory alive, and the 250th anniversary of the Lisbon earthquake was a roundly suggestive milestone. The city was host to an international seismology conference, many of whose participants regarded the journey to Lisbon as akin to a pilgrimage to the birthplace of their discipline. There were well-attended public lectures on the quake and its aftermath, an exhibition at the Museu de Arte Antiga dedicated to images of the disaster, and guided tours of the still burned-out Carmo Monastery. The Portuguese newspapers were full of glossy quake-related supplements, and local television aired a series of timely documentaries. The only thing missing, thank goodness, was a few tremors.

Just why the Lisbon earthquake became a watershed event in the Western world has as much to do with the severity of the human and material loss as it does with the historical time and place in which the calamity occurred. Modern seismologists estimate that the magnitude of the earthquake was approximately M=9 (Mercalli scale), that is to say, catastrophic. The epicenter of the quake was located southwest of Lisbon, about sixty miles offshore. In all, between fifteen and sixty thousand people lost their lives in Lisbon alone on account of the earthquake and the ensuing tsunamis and fire; tens of thousands more died elsewhere. As all-consuming as the disaster was, however, the shock waves that the earthquake caused in public opinion were due, to a large extent, to a few fortuitous particulars. A natural disaster of like proportions had not visited Europe, let alone a cosmopolitan capital city and a bustling port, in recorded memory; in the European consciousness, Lisbon was simply not far-off Lima, Peru, or peripheral Port au Prince, Haiti. Although the disaster struck large parts of Portugal, southern Spain, and North Africa, history, which is by nature selective, has come to regard the event as the Great Lisbon Earthquake. The timing too was laden with significance. The seismic disaster struck at nine-thirty in the morning, precisely when Lisbon's churches were chock full of worshippers in the midst of their devotions on one of the most solemn feasts in the liturgical calendar, All Saints' Day. Had the terror arrived a day before or a week later, the calamity would likely not have given rise to such a profound philosophical and theological debate.

Natural disasters are revelatory. The manner in which a society interprets a catastrophe and responds to the chaos exposes many of the accepted truths, prejudices, hopes, and fears of a culture suddenly and inexplicably confronted with ruin. In Lisbon's case, the disaster revealed a Portuguese society still firmly rooted in the old, absolute truths of God, Man, and Nature. That the Lisbon earthquake caused many of those inveterate truths to lose their reso-nance was one of the positive notes to arise from the ruins. The blow to the optimism of the Enlightenment was equally dev-astating. Had Lisbon not been laid waste, it is impossible to say if and when a similar tragedy would have prompted a Voltaire to question the notion that we live in the best of all possible worlds. After Lisbon, that world appeared to be suddenly and irrevocably transformed—God had ceased to be just and Nature to be beneficent—and everyone from staunch clerics to enlightened philosophers was compelled to reexamine his most cherished dogmas. The resultant speculation and debate left mankind slightly wiser. "Europe was joined together like a large family united by its differences. Europe's new woes seemed to be foretold by the earth-quakes felt in different parts of its territory, and so terribly in Lisbon, more than anywhere else," wrote Voltaire.[1] As for the official reaction to the chaos, the consummate government response, led by Carvalho, was an early attempt at disaster management, and given the scale of the death and destruction, the initiative was exceptionally efficient and far-sighted. The speed with which victims were buried and survivors fed was laudable; measures against pillage and profiteering were effective; and the reconstruction of the Baixa quarter, while protracted, provided Lisbon with a visionary urban plan that in more than two centuries has lost nothing of its practicality and aesthetic power.

Does the world then have something to learn from the legacy of Lisbon? In 1755 it took weeks for the news of the earthquake to travel by coach across Europe. Today we are besieged with news and images of natural disaster virtually in real time, and the catalog of catastrophe is horrific. In only a few years' time we have seen landslides in Kyrgyzstan, earthquakes in Iran and Pakistan, floods in Macedonia, mudslides in Nicaragua, locusts in West Africa, a typhoon in Japan, drought in Bolivia, a tsunami in South Asia, and a hurricane in New Orleans. In many instances these natural disasters generated an immense outpouring of funds, material aid, and goodwill—from governments and millions of individual donors, from church and civic groups, and from nongovernmental agencies—that attests to a deep-seated human need to pitch in when disaster strikes, as if something in our collective psyche is telling us that, who knows, we could be next. It has been said, with reason, that the "quiet" calamities of hunger and disease kill more of the world's poor than any tsunami or hurricane; but the fact remains that the dramatic spectacles that natural disasters unleash grip us in a peculiarly sentient way. The impulse may be morally questionable, but that doesn't make it any less true. The degree of official competence in confronting contemporary disasters is varied, but more than a few heads of state could learn a good deal from the decisiveness and determination of a Carvalho. Generally speaking, technologically advanced nations tend to fare better in the face of natural disasters, but not always. The Pacific Ocean, for example, is equipped with an early warning system against tsunamis, something that the Indian Ocean, rimmed by mostly poor nations, clearly lacks and that contributed to the alarmingly high death toll in the South Asia tsunami of 2004. But as Hurricane Katrina made tragically plain, even the most advanced societies will collapse in the event of a natural disaster when there is a scandalous lack of leadership, a breakdown of authority, and a widespread inability to rise to the occasion. Compared to New Orleans, Lisbon's record during the disaster seems positively exemplary.

Centuries have passed since the Great Lisbon Earthquake, and the world has witnessed scientific, industrial, and technological revolutions, but mankind has never managed to fully extricate God from the stage of natural disasters. In an interview on Al-Majd TV, an adviser to Saudi Arabia's justice minister explained the destruction of the South Asia tsunami thus: "Whoever reads the Koran, given by the Maker of the World, can see how these nations were destroyed. There is one reason: they lied, they sinned, and they are infidels. Whoever studies the Koran can see this is the result."[2] Nor is the age-old notion of a wrathful God confined exclusively to the Muslim world. The Most Reverend Philip M. Hannan, retired archbishop of New Orleans, was unequivocal in the wake of Katrina: "We are responsible as citizens for the sexual attitude, disregard of family rights, drug addiction, the killing of 45 million unborn babies, the scandalous behavior of some priests—so we have to understand that certainly the Lord has a right to chastisement . . . We have reached a depth of immorality that we have never reached before. And the chastisement was Katrina as well as Rita."[3] These moral exegeses applied to natural events are chillingly reminiscent of Malagrida, Wesley, and scores of other preachers from a past that many imagine to be good and buried. Perhaps our view of progress has grown exceedingly Panglossian. If Lisbon does indeed provide a lesson for the disasters that face us today, it is that man is at the center of our response to natural disaster, and not providence, metaphysics, or the ire of a living God.

NOTES

ONE: ALL SAINTS' DAY

1. John Wesley, *Serious Thought Occasioned by the Great Earthquake at Lisbon* (London, 1755).
2. Anonymous, *Description de la ville de Lisbonne* (Paris: Pierre Prault, 1730).
3. Rev. George Whitefield, *Works of the Reverend George Whitefield* (London: E. and C. Dilly, 1771).
4. Anonymous, *An account by an Eyewitness of the Lisbon Earthquake of November 1, 1755* (Lisbon: British Historical Society of Portugal, 1985), 24.
5. *Gentleman's Magazine* [London], 83 (February 1813), 105–6.
6. Ibid., 107.
7. Anonymous, *Account by an Eyewitness*, 10.
8. Ibid., 11.
9. Caetano Beirão, "Descrição Inédita do Terramoto de 1755 como o viu e viveu a Rainha D. Maria Victória," *Artes & Colecçoes* 1, no. 1 (June 1947), 3–4.

TWO: ORDER OUT OF CHAOS

1. Luís da Cunha, *Testamento político ou carta escrita pelo grande D. Luís da Cunha ao Senhor Rei D. José I* (Lisbon: Na Impressão Régia, 1820).
2. "A Particular Account of the Late, Dreadful Earthquake at Lisbon: With the Damage sustained by that Fatal Accident. In a letter from a gentleman of undoubted Veracity residing in Lisbon, to a Merchant in London, who publishes this early Account from a Principle of Benevolence, to satisfy the Curiosity of the Public," in Judite Nozes, trans., *The Lisbon Earthquake of 1755: British Accounts* (Lisbon: British Historical Society of Portugal, 1990).
3. J. J. Moreira de Mendonça, *História universal dos terramotos . . . com uma narraçam individual do terramoto do primeiro de Novembro de 1755* (Lisbon: Oficina de António Vicente da Silva, 1758), 145.
4. The original dispatch can be found in "State Papers, Portugal," Public Record Office, London.
5. Mendonça, *História universal*, 143.
6. Abraham Castres, letter in *Gentleman's Magazine* 25 (December 1755), 559.

7. F. L. Pereira de Sousa, *O terremoto do 1° de Novembro de 1755, e um estudo demográfico* (Lisbon: Serviços Geológicos de Portugal, 1932).
8. T. D. Kendrick, *The Lisbon Earthquake* (Philadelphia: Lippincott, 1956), 41.
9. Sousa, *O terremoto*, appendix.
10. Ibid., 92.
11. C. R. Boxer, *Some Contemporary Reactions to the Lisbon Earthquake of 1755* (Lisbon: Revista da Faculdade de Letras, 1956), 11.
12. Ibid., 14.
13. Ibid.

THREE: TAKING STOCK

1. F. L. Pereira de Sousa, *O terremoto do 1° de Novembro de 1755, e um estudo demográfico* (Lisbon: Serviços Geológicos de Portugal, 1932), 694.
2. Abraham Castres, letter in *Gentleman's Magazine* 25 (December 1755), 559.
3. *Gentleman's Magazine* 83 (February 1813), 105.
4. Castres, in *Gentleman's Magazine*, 559.
5. *Gentleman's Magazine* 83 (February 1813), 106.
6. Anonymous, *Account by an Eyewitness*, 12.

FOUR: ALIS UBBO . . . OLISIPO . . . AL-USHBUNA . . . LISBOA

1. Osbernus, *De expugnatione Lyxbonensi*, trans. C. W. David as *The Conquest of Lisbon* (New York: Columbia University Press, 2001), 111.
2. Ibid., 117.
3. Ibid., 123.
4. Ibid., 131.
5. Alvise da Cadamosto, "Description of Capo Dianco and the Islands Nearest to It," in J. H. Parry, *European Reconnaissance: Selected Documents* (New York: Walker, 1968), 60–61.

FIVE: A GOLDEN AGE, OF SORTS

1. John Foxe, *Book of Martyrs* (London: John Day, 1563).
2. Reverend John W. Dowling, *The History of Romanism: From the Earliest Corruptions of Christianity* (New York: E. Walker's Son, 1881), 21.
3. Stefan Zweig, *The Right to Heresy: Castellio against Calvin* (New York: Viking Press, 1936), 221–25.
4. The quotations from Voltaire's *Candide* come from *World Masterpieces*. Vol. 2, *Literature of Western Culture Through the Renaissance* (New York: Norton, 1956), 1312. In a footnote, the editors make the following comment on the translation: "*Abridged. 1759. Our text is the anonymous standard English translation of 1779–1781, with some changes by the present editor to make more evident Voltaire's wit and the brilliance of his style.*"
5. Sebastião José de Carvalho e Melo, *Discurso político sobre as vantagens que o Reino de Portugal pode alcançar da sua desgraça por ocasião de memo-*

rável terremoto de 1 de novembro de 1755 (Lisbon: Fundação Biblioteca Nacional, Manuscript Section, I, 12, 1, #14), 1–2.

SIX: THE PREACHER AND THE PHILOSOPHER

1. Johann Wolfgang von Goethe, *Aus meinem Leben: Dichtung und Wahrheit*, trans. Robert R. Heitner as *From My Life: Poetry and Truth* (Princeton: Princeton University Press, 1994), pt. 1.
2. Hester Lynch Piozzi, *Anecdotes of the Late Samuel Johnson, L.L.D.* (London, 1786).
3. Goethe, *From My Life.*
4. S. G. Tallentyre, *Voltaire in his Letters, being a Selection of His Correspondence* (New York: G. P. Putnam's Sons, 1919).
5. *The Portable Voltaire*, ed. Ben Ray Redman (New York: Viking Press, 1949).
6. Russell R. Dynes, *The Dialogue Between Voltaire and Rousseau on the Lisbon Earthquake: The Emergence of a Social Science View* (unpublished).
7. *The Collected Writings of Rousseau*, ed. Roger D. Masters and Christopher Kelly (Hanover, N.H.: University Press of New England, 1990), vol. 3, 110.
8. Voltaire, *Candide, or Optimism*, in *Portable Voltaire*, ed. Redman.
9. Ibid.
10. Ibid.
11. Ibid.
12. Fr. Gabriel Malagrida, *Juízo da verdadeira causa do terramoto* (Lisbon, 1756). Translation by the author.
13. *Gentleman's Magazine* 83 (February 1813), 105–6.
14. John Wesley, *Serious Thoughts Occasioned by the Great Earthquake at Lisbon* (London, 1755).
15. John Wesley, *Hymns Occasioned by the Earthquake, March 8, 1750. To which is added An Hymn upon the Pouring of the Seventh Vial. Occasioned by the Destruction of Lisbon* (Bristol, 1756).
16. T. D. Kendrick, *The Lisbon Earthquake* (Philadelphia: Lippincott, 1956), 161.
17. F. de Haes, *Het verheerlykte en vernederde Portugal*, quoted in Theo D'haen, "On how not to be Lisbon if you want to be modern—Dutch reactions to the Lisbon earthquake," *European Review* 14, no. 3 (2006), 352–53.
18. Benito Jerónimo Feijoo y Montenegro, *Nuevo systhema sobre la causa physica de los terremotos, explicado por los phenomenos eléctricos y adaptado al que padeció España en primero de Noviembre del año antecedente de 1755* (Puerto Santa Maria: Casa Real de las Cadenas, 1756).
19. John Rogers, "The Terribility, and the Moral Philosophy of Earthquakes," in *Three Sermons on Different Subjects and Occasions* (Boston: Edes and Gill, 1756), 48.
20. Ibid., 51.
21. Ibid., 47.
22. Ibid., 58.

23. Kendrick, *Lisbon Earthquake*, 73.
24. F. Aguilar Piñal, *Conmoción espiritual provocada en Sevilla por el terremoto de 1755* (Sevilla: Archivos Hispalenses, 1973).
25. Wesley, *Serious Thoughts*.

SEVEN: LIKE A PHOENIX FROM THE FLAMES

1. Anonymous, *An account by an Eyewitness of the Lisbon Earthquake of November 1, 1755* (Lisbon: British Historical Society of Portugal, 1985).
2. José Augusto França, *Lisboa Pombalina e o Iluminismo* (Lisbon: Bertrand Editora, 1983), 311.
3. Ibid., 327.
4. *Lettere famigliari di Giuseppe Baretti a' suoi tre fratelli tornando da Londra in Italia nel 1760* (Torino: M. Guigoni, 1857), 104–5.
5. Ibid., 109.

EIGHT: ENLIGHTENMENT AT ANY PRICE

1. Malagrida quoted in H. V. Livermore, *A New History of Portugal* (New York: Cambridge University Press, 1995), 227–28.
2. António Nunes Ribeiro Sanches, *Cartas sobre a educação da mocidade* (Porto: Domingos Barreira, n.d.), 25. Translation by the author.
3. António Nunes Ribeiro Sanches, *Obras* (Coimbra, 1959), 223. Translation by the author.
4. J. V. Serrão, *O Marquês de Pombal, O Homen, o Diplomata, e o Estadista* (Lisbon: Câmara Municipal de Lisboa, 1987), 22. Translation by the author.
5. Francisco de Lemos, *Relação geral do estado da universidad, 1772*, quoted in Kenneth Maxwell, *Pombal: Paradox of the Enlightenment* (New York: Cambridge University Press, 1995), 105.
6. Chevalier des Courtils, quoted in Maxwell, *Pombal*, 48.
7. António Henriques de Oliveira Marques, *History of Portugal* (New York: Columbia University Press, 1972), 1:385.
8. Lord Tyrawly, quoted in Maxwell, *Pombal*, 48.
9. Arthur William Costigan, *Sketches of Society and Manners in Portugal* (London, 1787), 2:29.
10. Nicolau Tolentino de Almeida, *Obras Completas* (Lisbon: Editores Castro, Irmão & Co., 1861), 274.
11. Paul Hazard, *European Thought in the Eighteenth Century from Montesquieu to Lessing* (New Haven, Conn.: Yale University Press, 1954).
12. Marcus Cheke, *Dictator of Portugal: A Life of the Marquis of Pombal, 1699–1782* (London: Sidgwick and Jackson, 1938), 72.

EPILOGUE

1. Voltaire quoted in Ana Cristina Araújo, "European Public Opinion and the Lisbon Earthquake," *European Review* 14, no. 3 (2006), 318.
2. The Middle East Media Research Institute, Special Dispatch Services, no. 842, January 7, 2005.
3. www.spiritdaily.org.

BIBLIOGRAPHY

There is no lack of correspondence, histories, sermons, and newspaper and journal accounts, as well as literary, scientific, and philosophical sources, pertaining to the Great Lisbon Earthquake. The disaster cast an exceedingly wide net, affecting theological and philosophical debate, seismological speculation, architecture and urban planning, international commerce, and political and social attitudes. Consequently the list of sources and research material is decidedly broad. I have worked from both Portuguese- and English-language texts; the latter are especially abundant due to the centuries-old ties between Britain and Portugal; the large and established British community in Lisbon at the time of the catastrophe, whose members bore witness to the destruction and whose testimony comprises a singular historical record; and the efforts of a generation of British historians, including Charles Ralph Boxer, David Birmingham, Kenneth Maxwell, and H. V. Livermore, among others, who have done much to bring the fascinating if relatively obscure history of diminutive Portugal to an English-speaking audience.

THE EARTHQUAKE: HISTORIES AND TESTIMONIES, CORRESPONDENCE AND DECREES

Anonymous. *An Account of the Late Dreadful Earthquake and Fire which destroyed the city of Lisbon, The Metropolis of Portugal. In a Letter from a Merchant Resident there, to his Friend in England.* London: J. Payne, 1755.

Beirão, C. "Descrição Inédita do Terramoto de 1755 como o viu e viveu a Rainha D. Maria Victória," *Artes & Colecçoes* 1, no. 1 (June 1947).

Boxer, C. R. *Some Contemporary Reactions to the Lisbon Earthquake of 1755.* Lisbon: Revista da Faculdade de Letras, 1956.

Castres, A., T. Chase, and anonymous authors. "Letters," *The Gentleman's Magazine* [London] (December 1755 and February, March, April 1813).

Conceição, C. da. *Em Que Se Dá Notícia Do Terremoto do 1° de Novembro.* Lisbon: Frenesi, 2005.

Fonseca, J. D. *1755, O terramoto de Lisboa*. Lisbon: Argumentum, 2004.

Gazeta de Lisboa, November 6, 1755.

Kendrick, T. D. *The Lisbon Earthquake*. Philadelphia: Lippincott, 1956.

Lisboa, A. P. de. *Memórias das Pricipais Providências que se Deram no Terremoto que Padeceu a Corte de Lisboa no Ano de 1755*. Lisbon, 1758.

Lodge, R. *The Private Correspondence of Sir Benjamin Keene*. New York: Cambridge, 1932.

Mendonça, J. J. Moreira de. *História universal dos terramotos que tem havido no mundo, de que há notícia, desde a sua creação até o século presente, com uma narraçam individual do terramoto do primeiro de Novembro de 1755, e notícia verdadeira dos seus effeitos em Lisboa, todo Portugal, Algarves, e mais partes da Europa, África, e América, aonde se estendeu . . .* Lisbon: Oficina de António Vicente da Silva, 1758.

Nozes, Judite, trans. *The Lisbon Earthquake of 1755: British Accounts*. Lisbon: British Historical Society of Portugal, 1990.

Portal, Fr. Manuel. *História da ruína da cidade de Lisboa causada pelo espantoso terramoto e incéndio que reduziu a pó e cinza a melhor e mayor parte desta infeliz cidade*. Lisbon, 1756.

Portugal, F., and A. Matos. *Lisboa em 1758, Memórias Paroquiais de Lisboa*. Lisbon: Publicações Culturais da Câmara Municipal de Lisboa, 1974.

Sousa, F. L. Pereira de. *O terremoto do 1° de Novembro de 1755, e um estudo demográfico*. Lisbon: Serviços Geológicos de Portugal, 1932.

PORTUGUESE HISTORY: EMPIRE AND COMMERCE, KINGS AND MINISTERS, ARCHAISM AND REFORM

Anonymous. *Description de la ville de Lisbonne*. Paris: Pierre Prault, 1730.

Beckford, W. *Italy, with Sketches of Spain and Portugal*. Paris: Baudry's European Library, 1834.

Birmingham, David. *A Concise History of Portugal*. New York: Cambridge University Press, 1993.

Boxer, C. R. *The Portuguese Seaborne Empire 1415–1825*. London: Hutchinson, 1969.

———. *The Church Militant and Iberian Expansion 1440–1770*. Baltimore: Johns Hopkins University Press, 1978.

Cadamosto, Alvise da. "Description of Capo Dianco and the Islands Nearest to It," in J. H. Parry, *European Reconnaissance: Selected Documents*. New York: Walker, 1968.

Carvalho e Melo, Sebastião José de. *Discurso político sobre as vantagens que o Reino de Portugal pode alcançar da sua desgraça por ocasião de memorável terremoto de 1 de novembro de 1755*. Lisbon: Fundação Biblioteca Nacional, Manuscript Section, I, 12, 1, #14.

Cheke, M. *Dictator of Portugal: A Life of the Marquis of Pombal, 1699–1782*. London: Sidgwick and Jackson, 1938.

Costigan, A.W. *Sketches of Society and Manners in Portugal*. London, 1787.

Cunha, Luís da. *Testamento político ou carta escrita pelo grande D. Luís da Cunha ao Senhor Rei D. José I.* Lisbon: Na Impressão Régia, 1820.

Fielding, H. *Journal of a Voyage to Lisbon.* London, 1755.

Figueiredo, A. Pereira de. *De Suprema Regum.* Lisbon, 1765.

Fisher, H. E. S. *The Portugal Trade: A Study of Anglo-Portuguese Commerce, 1700–1770.* London: Methuen, 1971.

Godinho, V. Magalhães. *A estrutura da antita sociedade Portuguesa.* Lisbon, 1975.

Hanson, C. A. *Economy and Society in Baroque Portugal, 1668–1703.* Minneapolis: University of Minnesota Press, 1981.

Herculano, A. *History of the Origin and Establishment of the Inquisition in Portugal.* New York: AMS Press, 1968.

Levenson, J., ed. *The Age of the Baroque in Portugal.* New Haven, Conn.: Yale University Press, 1993.

Ley, C. *Portuguese Voyages, 1498–1663.* London: Dent, 1953.

Livermore, H. V. *A History of Portugal.* New York: Cambridge University Press, 1947.

———. *Portugal and Brazil: An Introduction.* New York: Oxford University Press, 1953.

Macauley, R. *They Went to Portugal.* London: Jonathan Cape, 1946.

Macedo, J. Borges de. *Problemas de história da indústria Portuguesa no século XVIII.* Lisbon: Quereco, 1982.

Marques, A. H. Oliveira. *História de Portugal.* Lisbon: Imprensa Nacional, 1991.

Maxwell, K. *Pombal: Paradox of the Enlightenment.* New York: Cambridge University Press, 1995.

Osberrus, *De expugnatione Lyxbonnesi,* trans. C. W. David as *The Conquest of Lisbon.* New York: Columbia University Press, 2001.

Payne, S. G. *A History of Spain and Portugal.* Madison: University of Wisconsin Press, 1973.

Piozzi, H. L. *Anecdotes of the Late Samuel Johnson, L.L.D.* London, 1786.

Saraiva, A. J. *Inquisição e Cristãos-Novos.* Oporto, 1969.

Serrão, J. V. *O Marquês de Pombal, O Homen, o Diplomata, e o Estadista.* Lisbon: Câmara Municipal de Lisboa, 1987.

———. ed. *Dicionário de história de Portugal.* Lisbon, 1971.

Shaw, L. M. E. *Trade, Inquisition and the English Nation in Portugal, 1640–1690.* London: Carcancet, 1989.

Smith, J. A. [Conde de Carnota]. *Marquis of Pombal.* London, 1872.

Wheeler, D. L. *Historical Dictionary of Portugal.* New Jersey: Scarecrow Press, 1993.

THE THEOLOGICAL AND PHILOSOPHICAL DEBATE: PREACHERS AND PHILOSOPHERS, GOD'S WRATH, AND THE END OF OPTIMISM

Aguilar Piñal, F. *Conmoción spiritual provocada en Sevilla por el terremoto de 1755.* Archivos Hispalenses, 1973.

Brightman, E. S. "The Lisbon Earthquake: A Study of Religious Valuation." *American Journal of Theology* (1919).

Broome, J. H. *Rousseau, A Study of His Thought.* London: Edward Arnold, 1963.

Davidson, I. *Voltaire in Exile.* New York: Grove Press, 2004.

Dowling, Reverend J. W. *The History of Romanism: From the Earliest Corruptions of Christianity.* New York: E. Walker's Son, 1881.

Dynes, R. R. *The Dialogue Between Voltaire and Rousseau on the Lisbon Earthquake: The Emergence of a Social Science View.* Wilmington: University of Delaware. Unpublished.

————. *The Lisbon Earthquake in 1755: Contested Meanings in the First Modern Disaster.* Wilmington: University of Delaware, 1999. Unpublished.

Foxe, J. *Book of Martyrs.* London: John Day, 1563.

Gay, P. *The Enlightenment, an Interpretation.* New York: Knopf, 1966.

————. *Voltaire's Politics: The Poet as Realist.* New Haven, Conn.: Yale University Press, 1988.

Goethe, J. W. von. *Aus meinem Leber: Dichtung und Wahrheit,* trans. Robert R. Heitner as *From my Life: Poetry and Truth.* Princeton: Princeton University Press, 1994.

Grimsley, R. *Rousseau's Religious Writings.* Oxford: Clarendon Press, 1968.

Haes F. de. *Het verheerlykte en vernederde Portugal,* quoted in Theo D'haen, "On how not to be Lisbon if you want to be modem—Dutch reactions to the Lisbon earthquake," *European Review* 14, no. 3 (2006), 352–53.

Hazard, P. *European Thought in the Eighteenth Century from Montesquieu to Lessing.* New Haven, Conn.: Yale University Press, 1954.

Leibnitz, G. W. von. *The Philosophical Works of Leibnitz,* trans. George M. Duncan. New Haven, Conn.: Tuttle, Morehouse and Taylor, 1890.

Mack, M., ed. *Alexander Pope: An Essay on Man.* London: Routledge, 1993.

Malagrida, G. *Juízo da verdadeira causa do terramoto.* Lisbon, 1756.

Mason, H. *Candide, Optimism Demolished.* New York: Twayne Publishers, 1992.

Masters, R. D., and C. Kelly, eds. *The Collected Writings of Rousseau,* vol. 3. Hanover, N.H.: University Press of New England, 1990.

Piñal, F. Aguilar, *Conmoción espiritual provocada en Sevilla por el terremoto de 1755.* Sevilla: Archivos Hispalenses, 1973.

Piozzi, H. L. *Anecdotes of the Late Samuel Johnson, L.L.D.* London, 1786.

Redman, B. R., ed. *The Portable Voltaire.* New York: Viking Press, 1949.

Rogers, J. "The Terribility, and the Moral Philosophy of Earthquakes," in *Three Sermons on Different Subjects and Occasions.* Boston: Edes and Gill, 1756.

Sanches, A.N.R. *Cartas sobre a educação da mocidade.* Porto: Domingos Barreira, n.d.

Silva, J. Alvares de. *Investigação das causas proximas do terremoto, sucedido em Lisboa.* Lisbon, 1756.

Silva, J. Seabra da. *Dedução Cronológica e Analítica.* Lisbon, 1767.

Tallentyre, S. G. *Voltaire in his Letters, being a Selection of His Correspondence.* New York: G. P. Putnam's Sons, 1919.

Vernay, A. *Verdadeiro método de estudar.* Lisbon, 1746.

Voltaire. *Philosophical Dictionary.* Translated by H. I. Wolf. New York: Knopf, 1924.

———. *Candide*, in *World Masterpieces.* Vol. 2, *Literature of Western Culture Through the Renaissance.* New York: Norton, 1956.

Wade, I. O. *Voltaire and Candide: A Study of the Fusion of History, Art and Philosophy.* Princeton: Princeton University Press, 1959.

Wesley, J. *Serious Thoughts Occasioned by the Late Earthquake at Lisbon.* London, 1755.

———. *Hymns Occasioned by the Earthquake, March 8, 1750. To which is added An Hymn upon the Pouring of the Seventh Vial. Occasioned by the Destruction of Lisbon.* Bristol, 1756.

Whitefield, G. *Works of the Reverend George Whitefield.* London: E. and C. Dilly, 1771.

Wiley, B. *The Eighteenth Century Backround: Studies on the Idea of Nature in the Thought of the Period.* London: Chatto and Windus, 1940.

Zweig, S. *The Right to Heresy: Castellio against Calvin.* New York: Viking Press, 1936.

ARCHITECTURE AND URBANISM: ENGINEERS AND ENLIGHTENED URBAN PLANNING, MONUMENTS AND PALACES

Aires, C. *Manuel da Maia e os engenheiros militares portugueses no terremoto de 1755.* Lisbon, 1910.

Associação dos Archirectos Portugueses, ed. *Guia de Arquitectura, Lisboa '94.* Lisbon, 1994.

Castro, J. M. de. *Descrição analítica da execução da real estatua ecuestre do Señor Rei Fidelíssimo D. José I.* Lisbon, 1810.

França, J. A. *Lisboa Pombalina e o Iluminismo.* Lisbon: Bertrand, 1983.

———. *A reconstrução de Lisboa e a arquitectura pombalina.* Lisbon: Instituto de Cultura e Lengua Portuguesa, 1989.

Gideon, S. *Space, Time and Architecture.* Cambridge, Mass.: Harvard University Press, 1941.

Kaufmann, E. *Architecture in the Age of Reason.* Cambridge, Mass.: Harvard University Press, 1955.

Kubler, G. *Art and Architecture in Spain and Portugal and Their American Dominions, 1500–1800.* Harmondsworth: Penguin, 1959.

Pommer, R. *Eighteenth-Century Architecture in Piedmont: The Open Structures of Juvarra, Alfieri and Vittone.* New York: New York University Press, 1967.

Santos, L. R. *Monuments of Portugal.* Lisbon: National Secretariat of Information, 1940.

Sousa, F. L. Pereira de. *Efeitos do terremoto de 1755 nas construcções de Lisboa.* Lisbon, 1909.

Viterbo, S. *Diccionario histórico e documental dos arquitectos, engeneiros e construtores portugueses ou ao serviço de Portugal.* Lisbon, 1899–1922.

SEISMOLOGY: EARLY SPECULATIONS, BIRTH OF A NEW
SCIENCE, CONTEMPORARY ESTIMATES

Burnet, T. *The Sacred Theory of the Earth.* 1691; reprinted by Carbondale: Southern Illinois University Press, 1965.

Fuchs, K. "The Great Earthquakes of Lisbon 1755 and Aceh 2004 Shook the World: Seismologists' Societal Responsibility." Public Lecture, 250th anniversary of the 1755 Lisbon Earthquake, Lisbon.

Kant, I. *Geschichte und Naturbeschreibung der merkwürdigsten Vorfälle des Erdbebens, welches an dem Ende des 1755sten Jahres einen grossen Theil der Erde erschüttert hat.* Königsberg, 1756, republished in *Kants Werke I.* Berlin: Akademie Textausgabe, 1968.

Mallet, R. "On the Dynamics of Earthquakes; being an Attempt to reduce their observed Phenomeny to the known Laws of Wave Motion in Solids and Fluids. Read 9th February 1848." *Irish Academy* 21 (1848), 51–113.

Mendonça, J. J. Moreira de. *História universal dos terremotos que tem havido no mundo, de que há notícia, desde a sua creação até o século presente, com uma narraçam individual do terremoto do primeiro de Novembro de 1755, e notícia verdadeira dos seus effeitos em Lisboa, todo Portugal, Algarves, e mais partes da Europa, África, e América, aonde se estendeu.* Lisbon: Oficina de António Vicente da Silva, 1758.

Michell, J. "Conjectures concerning the Cause of Observations upon the Phaenomena of Earthquakes," *Philosophical Transactions of the Royal Society* 51 (1760), 566–634.

Reid, H. F. "The Lisbon Earthquake of November 1, 1755." *Bulletin of the Seismological Society of America* 4 (1979).

Reinhardt, O., and D. R. Oldroyd. "Kant's Theory of Earthquakes and Volcanic Action." *Annals of Science* 40, no. 3 (May 1983).

Richter, C. *Elementary Seismology.* San Francisco: Freeman, 1958.

Zitelini, N., et al. "The Tectonic Source of the 1755 Lisbon Earthquake and Tsunami." *Annali di Geofisica* 42 (1999).

INDEX

Abrantes, Marquês de, 34
Academia dos Ilustrados, 27–28
Academia Real da História Portuguesa,
    28, 29
Afonso, king of Portugal, 68–69, 70,
    72–73
Africa, 76–79, 87, 104
Age of Discovery, 6, 57, 67, 75–77,
    83–85
Age of Reason, 111–12
Alegrete, Marquês de, 37–38, 191
Alfama, 67n, 75
All Saints' Day, 5, 12–13, 206
Almeida, Nicolau Tolentino de, 196
American Revolution, 200
Anglicans, 134
anti-Catholicism, 132, 134, 143
anti-Semitism, 86–87, 88, 97
architecture, 85, 156, 162, 201
Aristotle, 139, 141
Asia, 83, 84, 86, 87, 100, 104
Atoguia, Conde de, 172, 174
Aula do Comércio, 181
Austria, 30
Austrian Succession, War of the, 32n
Aveiro, Duque de (José de
    Mascarenhas), 172, 173, 174

Bacon, Francis, 136, 138, 140
Baixa Pombalina, 166, 201
Baixa quarter, 192–95, 201; Carvalho
    honored in renaming of, 166;
    clearance of shantytown in, 159;

destruction of, 54, 150, 151–52;
    earthquake proofing used in
    reconstruction of, 164–65;
    legalities in reconstruction of,
    162–63; new street names and
    guilds assigned for, 166;
    pre-earthquake descriptions of,
    150, 151, 161–62; prefabrication
    used in reconstruction of, 164;
    reconstruction of, 154–68,
    191–92, 207
Barcelona, 165
Baretti, Giuseppe, 167–68
Baschi, M. de, 46
Beckford, William, 200n
Belém, 34n, 42, 59, 85, 109, 150,
    154–55, 171; executions held at,
    173–74; royal family at, 20–24,
    39–40, 47, 61
Belém, Tower of, 173, 176
Benedict XIV, Pope, 107, 175–76
Berlinische Nachrichten, 115–16
Birmingham, David, 181n
Black Legend, 89, 134, 179
Book of Martyrs (Foxe), 89–90, 93
Boxer, Charles, 10n
Brazil, 6–7, 8, 34, 44, 59, 83–84, 85,
    100, 104, 105–6, 108, 160, 177,
    186, 188; gold from, 6–7, 21, 34,
    105–6, 107, 110–11, 186, 189,
    190; independence of, 200;
    Portugal's colonization of, 83–84;
    Portugal's dependence on, 59, 84,

Brazil (*cont.*)
    186–87; royal family's flight to,
    200; slavery as economic necessity
    in, 185
British Factory, 12, 52, 136
British Merchant, 187
Buchanan, George, 96–97

Cabral, Pedro Álvars, 83
Cadamosto, Alvise da, 78
Calvin, John, 94–95
Calvinism, 130
Câmara d'Atalaia, José Cardinal
    Manuel da, 38–39, 131
Camões, Luís de, 81
Candide (Voltaire), 3, 123–27
Carmo Monastery, 206
Carvalho, Paulo, 191, 193
Carvalho e Melo, Sebastião José de
    (Marquês de Pombal): authority
    for postearthquake response and
    reconstruction given to, 24;
    background and rise to power of,
    27–31, 173; Baixa Pombalina
    named in honor of, 166; Baixa's
    new street names assigned by, 166;
    biographers of, 198–99; bronze
    medallion cast in honor of, 194,
    197, 200; "bury the dead" advice
    of, 24, 34; as chief of police, 186;
    death of, 197; as despotic ruler,
    159, 165–66, 174, 179–80, 196,
    198–99; earthquake as viewed by,
    111–12; educational reforms of,
    181–84, 191, 199; enemies of,
    159–60, 163, 172, 173, 191,
    195–96; as Estrangeirado,
    139–40, 144; fall from power of,
    195–97; in immediate aftermath
    of earthquake, 31–41;
    industrialization campaign of,
    189–90, 191, 199; Jesuits opposed
    and expelled by, 129, 174–77, 191;
    José I as protector of, 41, 131–32,
    160, 195; legacy of, 191, 199;
    Lisbon reconstruction overseen by,
    153, 155, 157, 159–61, 165–66;
    Malagrida as enemy of, 129,
    131–32, 177–79; monument
    erected to, 201; reform priorities

and philosophy of, 161, 162,
    166, 179–80, 183–86, 190;
    rehabilitated reputation of, 199,
    200–201; repeal of reforms of, 196,
    197; retribution for plotters against
    King José overseen by, 171–74;
    seismological questionnaire
    published by, 144–46; social
    reforms of, 184–86, 191, 199;
    titles given to, 174, 190–91;
    two sides to rule of, 197–99
Carvalho e Mendonça, Paulo de, 178
Casa da India, 12, 17, 84, 151, 161
Casa do Risco (Drafting House), 162,
    163, 165
Castelo de São Jorge, 5, 32, 66
Castres, Abraham, 36–37, 40, 43,
    47, 52
Catarina, queen of Portugal, 98
Catarina de Bragança, Princess, 104–5,
    143
Catholic Church, *see* Roman Catholic
    Church
censorship, 96, 182–83
Cerdá, Ildefonso, 165
Cevallos, José de, 136–37
Charles I, king of England, 104
Charles II, king of England, 104, 143,
    158
charter companies, 190, 197
Chase, Thomas, 15–17, 131
Cheke, Marcus, 199
Christianity, 66, 68, 71, 73–75; *see also*
    Protestants; Roman Catholic
    Church
Clement XIII, Pope, 176, 177
Clement XIV, Pope, 177*n*
Coimbra, 23, 36, 155, 174
Coimbra, University of, 28, 96–97,
    103, 109, 139, 169, 175, 183
Colbert, Jean-Baptiste, 30
Concise History of Portugal, A
    (Birmingham), 181*n*
*Conjectures concerning the Cause of
    Observations upon the Phaenomena
    of Earthquakes* (Michell), 142
Conquest of Lisbon, The (Osbernus), 63,
    70–71, 73
Cortes (Portuguese Parliament), 98,
    100, 101–2, 106

Costigan, Arthur William, 189
Counter-Reformation, 11, 13, 97, 179
Courtils, Chevalier des, 187
Crónica (Goes), 84
Crusades, 69, 72–73, 74, 75, 98, 107
Customs Exchange (Customs House),
    11, 17, 34, 54, 55, 160, 161–62,
    193

da Cunha, Cardinal, 195
da Cunha, Luís, 31
da Gama, Vasco, 83, 84, 87
d'Alembert, Jean le Rond, 141
Daun, Count Leopold Joseph von, 30
Daun, Leonara Ernestine, 30–31
de Haes, Frans, 134–35
Descartes, René, 138, 140
Description de la ville de Lisbonne, 8–9
diamonds, 6–7, 55, 59, 105, 106, 186
Dichtung und Wahrheit (Goethe),
    118–19
*Discovery and Plaine Declaration of
    Sundry Subtill Practices of the
    Holy Inquisition of Spain, A*
    (Montanus), 90
Dissertação (Maia), 153–55, 158, 160–61
Dominus ac Redemptor (Clement XIV),
    177n

earthquakes, 44, 141, 155, 206, 208;
    building design and, 164–65
education, 7, 10, 109; Carvalho's
    reforms in, 181–84, 191, 199;
    Jesuits' control of, 97–98, 138–39,
    140, 182
Enlightenment, 8, 28, 30, 115, 156, 207
Ericeira, Conde de, 28, 29, 189
Essais de théodicée . . . (Leibniz), 115
Essay on Man, An (Pope), 113
Estado Novo dictatorship, 201
Estrangeirados, 139–40, 144, 157, 186
Évora, University of, 176

Faria e Sousa, Manuel, 84
Feijoo y Montenegro, Benito Jerónimo,
    136–37
Felipe II, king of Spain, 99–100, 108
Felipe IV, king of Spain, 102
Fernando, king of Spain, 87
Fernando VI, king of Spain, 46

fidalgos, 27, 191
Fielding, Henry, 147, 149–50
Figueireda, António Pereira de, 129
Fonseca, Gualter da, 157, 160
Foxe, John, 89–90, 93
France, 46, 79, 89, 101, 102, 103–4,
    106, 107, 110, 117, 177n, 196, 200
French Revolution, 179, 193n, 200

gaiolas, 164–65
Gaspar, Prince, 36, 107
Gazeta de Lisboa, 41, 115, 172
Gazette de France, 116
Geneva, 94–95, 119, 122, 123–24
Genovesi, Antonio, 138
Gentleman's Magazine, 53, 142
George, Saint, 20
George II, king of England, 45, 131, 180
Germanic tribes, 6, 66, 73, 75
Germany, 110, 117, 131, 159
Gilbert of Hastings, 74
Girardon, François, 193
Goes, Damião de Goes, 84
Goethe, Johann Wolfgang von, 117
gold, 6, 21, 34, 45–46, 55, 58–60, 62,
    77, 105–6, 107, 110–11, 186,
    189, 190
Gold Coast (Ghana), 77
Graevenhaegse Courant, 116
Great Britain, 10, 79, 117, 158–59;
    Portuguese Jews in exile in, 185,
    186; and religious views on
    earthquakes, 132–34, 143; *see also*
    merchants, British; Portuguese-
    British relations
Great Lisbon Earthquake: aftershocks
    and other earthquakes after,
    42–43, 44n, 152; aid sent to
    Portugal after, 45–47, 61; annual
    remembrance ceremony conducted
    for, 205; burials conducted at sea
    after, 38–39; criminality in
    aftermath of, 32–35, 41, 53;
    damage done by, 54–58, 111, 135,
    150, 151–52, 166–68, 192; date
    and time of, 5, 12, 14, 206; death
    toll in, 41, 43, 51–53, 150, 206;
    destruction directly due to shocks
    of, 17–18; economic toll of,
    55–57; engraved illustrations of,

Great Lisbon Earthquake (*cont.*)
117–18; epicenter of, 206;
establishment of order after,
34–36; exodus from Lisbon after,
31–32, 39; eyewitness accounts of,
14–17, 19–20, 33–34, 116–17;
fires after, 18–20, 31, 32, 34, 35,
38, 51, 54, 55, 206; first official
report published about, 41, 115;
food distribution after, 37–38, 47;
historical comparisons to, 53–54;
legacy of, 208–9; magnitude of,
206; number of shocks in, 13–14,
17; as opportunity for renewal,
156; *optimisme* vs. reason and,
111–12, 113–27, 207; other
locations affected by, 43–44,
206; religious reactions to, 1–2,
39, 46, 54, 58, 60, 62, 118–19,
128–36, 206; scientific responses
to, 136–46; spreading of news
about, 115–18, 208; tsunamis
after, 20, 23, 43–44, 51, 55,
58, 206
Great London Fire, 143, 154, 158
guilds, 166

Hamburg, 46, 57, 131
Hannan, Philip M., 209
Haussmann, Baron, 165
Hazard, Paul, 199
Henrique, Prince, 98
Henry the Navigator, Prince, 6, 75,
76, 78
heretics, 88–95, 186
Herrera, Juan de, 12
Herring, Thomas, 134
High Gothic Manueline style, 85
História de Portugal (Oliveira Martins),
203
História universal dos terramotos . . .
(Moreira), 25
*History and Natural Descriptions of the
noteworthy events of the Earthquake
. . .* (Kant), 140–41
Hobbes, Thomas, 30
Holy Week, 88
Hooke, Robert, 141
Hospital de Todos os Santos, 151
Hume, David, 140, 143

Ignacio, San, 175
India, 83, 84, 105, 172
industrialization, 189–90, 191, 199
Inquisition, Holy Office of the, 10,
11–12, 28, 88–97, 111, 137;
autos-da-fé of, 11, 89, 91–93, 96;
Candide and, 124, 125–26;
censorship conducted by, 96;
censorship power stripped from,
182; as civil court, 186; Crown's
revision of sentences passed by, 129;
earthquake's damage to, 135; end
of, 96; establishment in Portugal
of, 11, 88, 89, 96, 98; headquarters
of, 18, 54, 151; Jews targeted by,
88, 92, 96; Malagrida brought
before, 178–79; number of victims
of, 96; in Spain, 89, 93, 96; use of
torture by, 89, 90–91, 96, 135
*Investigação das causes proximas do
terramoto, succedido em Lisboa*
(Silva), 136
Isabel, queen of Spain, 87
Islam: Christian conversions to, 68; *see
also* Muslims
Italy, 7

Japan, 165
Jerónimos Monastery, 85, 149
Jesuits (Society of Jesus), 13, 102, 128;
Carvalho as enemy of, 129, 160,
172, 174–77, 181; confiscation
of wealth of, 175–76, 181;
dissolution and other countries'
expulsions of, 177n; education
under control of, 97–98, 138–39,
140, 182; expelled from Portugal
by Carvalho, 176–77, 181, 191;
founder of, 175; plot against king
José and, 172, 173
Jews, 17; Carvalho's ending of
institutional discrimination
against, 185–86; conversion to
Christianity of, 11, 86, 87–88,
185; emigration of, 88; in exile, 30,
110, 131, 185; expulsion from
Spain, 87; under Muslim rule,
66–67; persecution of, 30, 92, 96,
111; in Portuguese society, 86–87
João, Prince, 200

João III, king of Portugal, 98
João IV, king of Portugal, 103, 104
João V, king of Portugal, 6, 29, 30, 36,
     45n, 57, 60, 106–11, 128, 131,
     140, 157
John (archbishop of Braga), 70–71, 74
Johnson, Samuel, 117
Jorge, São, 20
José, Prince, 36, 107
José I, king of Portugal, 31, 40–41,
     47, 59, 61, 150, 156, 160, 198;
     birth of, 108; Carvalho given
     postearthquake command by, 24;
     Carvalho given titles by, 174,
     190–91; as Carvalho's protector,
     41, 131–32, 160, 195; death of,
     181, 195; in earthquake, 20–24;
     equestrian statue of, 162, 192–94,
     195, 197, 200; *Fidelissimus* title
     of, 10; illegitimate sons of, 174;
     Malagrida sent into internal exile
     by, 131–32; masonry-sustained
     roofs avoided by, 192; nobles' plot
     against, 171–74, 176, 196; royal
     decree for rebuilding of Lisbon
     issued by, 162–63; royal possessions
     of, 34n
Journal Étranger, 116–17
Journal of a Voyage to Lisbon (Fielding),
     147, 149
Judaizers, 92, 186
Juderías, 86
Juvarra, Filippo, 158

Kant, Immanuel, 140–51, 183
Katrina, Hurricane, 208–9
Keene, Sir Benjamin, 43, 45
King, Charles, 187
Kjobenhavns ridende Post, 116

Latin America, 159, 175
Le Bas, Jacques Philippe, 118
Le Brun, Charles, 193
Leibniz, Gottfried Wilhelm von, 115,
     118, 120, 124
Lemos, Francisco de, 183–84, 197
Lettere familiari di Giuseppe Baretti . . .
     (Baretti), 167–68
Letters on the Education of Young People
     (Sanches), 182

Lisbon: abandonment considered for,
     23, 24, 36, 40–41, 150–51,
     154–55; in Age of Discovery, 85;
     aqueduct of, 60, 109–10, 153,
     157; barrios of, 152; Carvalho's
     monument in, 201; Carvalho's
     remains reburied in, 200–201;
     City Senate of, 38, 157, 191, 193;
     clergy and churches of, 9–11, 39,
     52, 58, 60, 128, 129, 159–60, 162,
     200; descriptions and history of,
     5–9, 62, 65, 109–10, 147, 149–50;
     earthquake of 1755 in, *see* Great
     Lisbon Earthquake; Fielding in,
     147, 149–50; foreign visitors eager
     to see ruins of, 166–68, 192;
     Maia's plans for rebuilding of,
     152–55; mestizo society in, 79;
     under Muslim rule, 66–75; patron
     saint of, 12; pogrom in, 88, 111;
     population of, 7, 10, 51–52; in
     Reconquest, 12, 68–75; royal
     decree issued for rebuilding of,
     162–63; seismology conference
     held in, 205–6; sixteenth-century
     earthquake in, 155; slaves in,
     78–79; sources of funds for
     rebuilding of, 159–60; strategic and
     commercial importance of, 44–45,
     55, 65, 69; *see also* Baixa quarter
Lisbon Basalt Complex, 155n
Lobo da Cunha, António de Santa
     Marta, 183
Locke, John, 30, 138, 140, 183
London, 10, 29–30, 31, 44, 45, 47, 53,
     57, 130–31, 139, 143, 152, 154,
     158; Carvalho's diplomatic posting
     in, 29–30, 186, 189
London Gazette, 142
London Magazine, 116
Louis XIV, king of France, 104, 193
Louis XV, king of France, 46
Louriçal, Marquês de, 57, 138
Lusiads, The (Camões), 81
Luther, Martin, 94

Machado de Castro, Joaquim, 193–94
Mafra palace-convent, 108, 128
Maia, Manuel da, 60, 152–59, 164,
     165; background and career of,

Maia, Manuel da (*cont.*)
152–53, 156; collaborating
architects selected by, 157; death
of, 191; plans for rebuilding Lisbon
presented by, 152–55, 160–61
Malagrida, Gabriel, 113, 128–29, 131,
136, 138, 144, 183, 209; Carvalho
as enemy of, 129, 131–32, 172,
177–79, 198–99; imprisonment
and execution of, 177–79, 196,
198–99; jailhouse writings of, 178;
pamphlet on earthquake published
by, *see Opinion on the True Cause of
the Earthquake, An*; plot against
King José and, 172, 173, 176;
sent into internal exile, 131–32
Malik, Abd Al-, 99
Mallet, Robert, 142
Manuel I, king of Portugal, 83, 84, 85,
87, 98, 100, 151
Mardel, Carlos, 60, 140, 153, 157, 160,
162, 165, 191
Maria I, queen of Portugal, 195–96,
197, 200
Maria Ana, queen of Portugal, 30–31,
47, 108
Maria Ana, Victória, queen of Portugal,
20, 21–22, 195–96
Maria Barbara, Princess, 46
Marranos, *see* New Christians
Maxwell, Kenneth, 198
Mazarin, Cardinal, 104
mercantilism, 187, 189
merchants, 54–55, 102, 109, 110, 156,
186; British, 7, 12, 15, 18–20, 44,
52–53, 55–57, 110, 131, 188–89;
Carvalho's relationship with,
159–60, 173, 179; Dutch, 88
mestizos, 79
Methodism, 132
Methuen, Treaty of (1703), 110,
187, 189
Michell, John, 141–42, 143
Mint, 34, 54, 58–59
"Mohocks," 29
monarchism, 180
Montanus, Reginaldus, Gonsalvus, 90
Moreira de Mendonça, Joaquim José,
25, 35, 38
Morocco, 43–44, 75–76, 98–99, 105

Mosaic Law, 93–94
Moses, 131
Mota, Cardinal, 29
Museu de Arte Antiga, 205
Muslims, 66–75, 209; cultural
contributions of, 67–68, 74;
expulsion from Spain of, 87;
Portugal under rule of, 66–68; and
Reconquest of Portugal, 68–75;
religious tolerance under, 66–67

Naples, 142, 155, 177n
"natural philosophers," 142
Netherlands, 7, 44, 46–47, 79, 88,
101, 103–4, 105, 110, 116, 117,
130, 185
New Christians (Marranos), 11, 87–88,
99, 139–40, 179, 185–86, 199
New England, 137
New Orleans, La., 208–9
Newton, Sir Isaac, 30, 140, 143
Nicholas V, Pope, 77
nobility, 27, 52, 87, 102–3, 109; Baixa
reconstruction opposed by, 163;
Carvalho as enemy of, 159–60,
173, 174, 181; monopolies on
imports held by, 6–7; in plot
against King José, 171–74, 196;
restoration of power of, 197; status
of, 27
noblesse de robe, 28
Noronha e Bourbon, Teresa, 29–30
novos homens, 183–84
*Nuevo systhema sobere la causa physica
de los terremotos* (Feijoo), 136
Nunes, Pedro, 85

"Occasioned by the Death of Mr. G.
Vincent . . . ," 53
Olivares, Duque de, 102
Oliveira Martins, Joaquim Pedro de,
203
*Opinion on the True Cause of the
Earthquake, An* (Malagrida), 113,
129–30, 132, 177, 183
optimisme vs. reason, 111–12, 113–27,
207
Order of Christ, 76
Osbernus (Osbern of Bawdsey), 63,
70–71, 73

Paço da Ribeira, 17, 20, 34n, 54, 103, 151, 167–68
Palácio dos Estaus, 18, 135
"Palhava Boys," 174
Panglossian, 126, 209
Papal States, 176
Paris, 116, 159, 165, 193
Parma, 177n
Pedegache, Miguel Tibério, 116–17, 118
Pedro V, king of Portugal, 200
Pele, Giovanni Battista, 191
Pennsylvania Gazette, 55
Perelada, Conde de, 46
Pinto, Isaac de, 88n
plague, 38, 62, 86
Poème sur le désaster de Lisbonne (Voltaire), 120–22, 126
Political Discourse . . . , A (Carvalho), 111–12
political eligibility, 185, 199
Pombal, 197, 201
Pombal, Marquês de, *see* Carvalho e Melo, Sebastiâo José de
Pombal (Maxwell), 198
Pombal Survey, 144–46
Pope, Alexander, 113, 115, 118
Poppe, Elias Sebastiao, 157, 160, 162
Portal, Manuel, 42, 51
Portugal: Carvalho's modernization of, 183–84; Church's power in, 8–11, 39, 75; fleet of, 60; France's invasion of, 200; lack of resources in, 7; medieval character of, 97, 139, 180, 207; under Muslim rule, 66–68; parliament of, *see* Cortes; patron saint of, 20; population of, 86; post-Carvalho misfortunes of, 199–200; Reconquest of, 68–75; undoing of Carvalho's reforms in, 196, 197
"Portugal Glorified and Humiliated" (de Haes), 134–35
Portuguese-British relations, 44, 103; earthquake relief, 45, 47; military, 29, 101, 105, 187, 189, 200; royal intermarriages, 104–5; trade, 29, 45, 110, 187–90
Portuguese Empire, 6–7, 8, 44, 76–79, 83–86, 98, 100, 101, 105–6;

Portugal's dependence on, 59, 84, 186–87
Portuguese-Spanish relations, 41, 44, 105, 106; earthquake relief and, 46; periods of unification in, 61, 99–102; Portuguese rebellion, 101–3, 151; royal intermarriage and, 46
Praça do Comércio, 192–93, 197
Protestants, 2, 10, 17, 19, 46, 89–90, 92–96, 128, 132, 134–36, 185
Proverbs, Book of, 111
Public Advertiser, 142

"Quixotada, A" (Almeida), 196

Real Mesa Censória, 182
Robinson, Sir Thomas, 36
Rogers, John, 137–38
Roman Catholic Church, 1–2, 106; anti-Semitism fostered by, 87; Carvalho's power struggle with, 175; Carvalho's rebuilding of Lisbon opposed by, 159–60, 162; illegitimate children of master-slave unions baptized into, 79; power of, 8–11, 39, 75; restoration of power of, 197, 200; separated from state, 180, 191; slave trade sanctioned by, 77; Voltaire's attacks on, 120, 124; wealth of, 6; *see also* anti-Catholicism; Inquisition, Holy Office of the; Lisbon, clergy and churches of
Roman Empire, 5–6, 65–66, 71, 75
Romanus Pontifex (Nicholas V), 77
Rousseau, Jean-Jacques, 122–23
"royal fifth," 6, 21
Royal Palace, 161
ruas nobres, 160–61, 162

St. Paul's Cathedral, 158
Salazar, António de Oliveira, 201
Saldanha, Cardinal, 175–76
Salem, Mass., 95
Salvi, Nicola, 107
Sampaiò, Monsignor, 36
san benitos, 91–92
Sanches, António Ribeiro, 140, 144, 182

Santa Clara, Joachim de, 197
Santos, António Ribeiro dos, 169, 199
Santos, Eugénio dos, 157, 160–62, 163–65, 166, 191, 193
São Domingos, Church of, 135
São Roque, Church of, 107–8
São Vincente de Fora, 12–13
Saudi Arabia, 209
science, 182, 183; in responses to earthquake, 136–46
Sebastião, king of Portugal, 98–99
Sé Cathedral, 34, 36, 52, 74
Second Crusade, 69, 74
seismology, 141–42, 144–46; 2005 conference on, 205–6
Senado da Câmara, 38
Serious Thoughts Occasioned by the Late Earthquake at Lisbon (Wesley), 132–34
Servetus, Michael, 95
slaves, slavery, 6, 8, 53, 74–75, 77–79, 84, 86, 87, 105; Carvalho's outlawing of, 185, 186, 191, 199
Society of Jesus, see Jesuits
Sousa Mexia, Bartolomeu de, 59
Southwell, Edward, 167
Spain, 43, 87, 89, 93, 96, 107, 139, 159, 196; Jesuits expelled from, 177n; see also Portuguese-Spanish relations
Spinoza, Baruch, 88n

Tagus River, 5, 18–29, 38, 39, 60, 62, 65, 83, 149, 150, 155, 162, 174
Tavares, José Acúrsio de, 49
Távora, Francisco de Assis, Marquês de, 171–74
Távora, Luis Bernardo de, 173
Távora, Manuel Varejão de, 135
Távora, Marquesa de, 171, 172, 173–74
Távora family, 171–74, 196, 198
Terreiro do Paço, 157, 160–62, 165

"Terribility, and the Moral Philosophy of Earthquakes, The" (Rogers), 137–38
Terzi, Filipo, 12–13
Texeira, Pedro, 171
textile industry, 187, 189
Thirty Years' War, 102
Thomas Aquinas, Saint, 97
Tomar, Council of, 100, 101
Tronchin, Jean-Robert, 119
True Method of Study (Verney), 140, 182
Turin, 158, 167

urban planning, 156, 158–59, 165, 201, 207

Vanvitelli, Luigi, 107
Vasco, Grão, 85
Verney, Luís António, 140, 144, 182
Vicente Gil, 84
Vieira, Custódio, 60, 153
Vienna, 30, 139, 140, 180
Vincent, Giles, 52–53
Vincent, Saint, 12
Viradeira, 196
Vittorio Amedeo II, Duke of Savoy and King of Sicily, 158
Voltaire, 3, 107, 119–27, 166, 183, 207

Walpole, Sir Robert, 180
wave propagation theory, 141
Wesley, John, 6, 111, 132–34, 135, 143–44, 209
Whitefield, George, 10–11, 143
wine industry, 187–88, 190
witches, 95
Wood, John, the Elder, 158–59
Wren, Christopher, 154, 158

Zacuto, Abraham ben Samuel, 87